Geoarchaeology

Using Earth Sciences to Understand the Archaeological Record

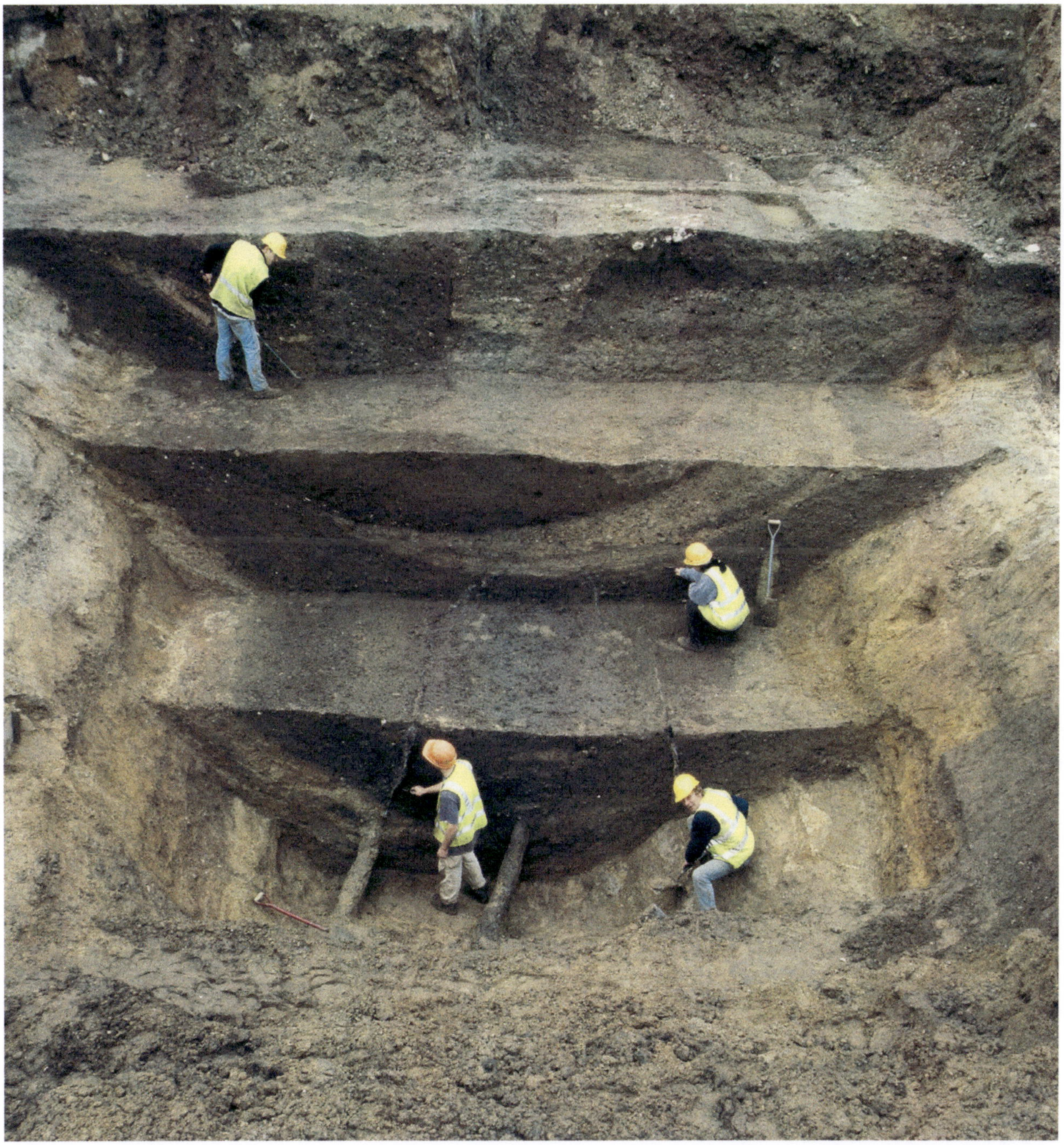

Summary

This guidance document covers the use of geoarchaeology to assist in understanding the archaeological record. Geoarchaeological techniques may range in scale from landscape studies to microscopic analysis, and are carried out by practitioners with specialist knowledge about the physical environment in which archaeological stratigraphy is preserved, and excavations take place. The main aim is usually to understand site formation processes, but there may also be issues concerning site preservation, refining field interpretations of archaeological contexts and identifying changes in the physical landscape through time.

Previous editions of this document were compiled in 2004 and 2007 by Gianna Ayala, Matthew Canti, Jen Heathcote, Raimonda Usai and Jane Siddell. This edition was revised in 2015 by Matthew Canti with help from Jane Corcoran.

First published by English Heritage 2004

Revised and reprinted by English Heritage 2007

This edition published by Historic England December 2015
All images © Historic England unless otherwise stated

HistoricEngland.org.uk/research/approaches/research-methods/archaeology/geoarchaeology/

Front cover
Section across the ditch of the south bailey at Norwich Castle.
© Norwich Archaeological Unit

Contents

Introduction 1

1 Site Formation Processes and Deposits 2

1.1 Slope processes and colluvial deposits 2
1.2 Alluvial processes and deposits 5
1.3 Aeolian processes and wind-blown deposits 9
1.4 Wetland processes and deposition 11
1.5 Marine and coastal deposits 14
1.6 Agricultural processes and deposits 15
1.7 Wastes and construction material accumulations 16
1.8 Soil development 18

2 Geoarchaeological Approaches to Stratigraphy 22

2.1 Field description and interpretation 22
2.2 Recognising depositional environments: basic descriptive criteria 23
2.3 Coring 26
2.4 Soil phosphorus analysis 30
2.5 Multi-element geochemical analysis........ 33
2.6 Micromorphology 35
2.7 X-radiography 36
2.8 Mineralogy 37
2.9 Particle size analysis 37
2.10 Loss on ignition 38
2.11 Magnetic susceptibility 39
2.12 pH 39
2.13 Typical geoarchaeological questions 41

3 Project Organisation and Planning 43

3.1 Planning and costs 43
3.2 Geoarchaeology at different stages of a project 44
3.3 Desk-top assessment 44
3.4 Evaluation 44
3.5 Excavation 45
3.6 Assessment 45
3.7 Analysis 45
3.8 Dissemination and archiving 46

4 Where to Get Advice 47

4.1 The Regional Science Advisors are currently (2015) 47

Appendix 1: Methods 49

A1 Finger texturing 49
A2 Troels-Smith description 49
A3 Magnetic susceptibility 50

Appendix 2: Glossary of Terms 53

Bibliography 56

Acknowledgements 59

Introduction

Geoarchaeology is the application of earth science principles and techniques to the understanding of the archaeological record. It is essentially an approach to archaeology, carried out by practitioners with specialist knowledge about the physical environment in which archaeological stratigraphy is preserved, and excavations take place. This knowledge can be used at a wide range of scales. It may cover issues of landscape change on the one hand, while examining microscopic context definitions on the other. In addition to these variations of scale, geoarchaeological analysis can also involve indirect studies complementing other specialist analyses (eg studying the stratigraphic integrity of a pollen sample sequence using micromorphology), examining taphonomy and residuality (eg burial conditions in relation to artefact recovery), and studies of the potential for site preservation.

Geoarchaeological approaches can thus assist many levels of archaeological enquiry, but are used chiefly for prospection, understanding site formation processes, explaining issues of preservation, refining field interpretations of archaeological contexts and identifying changes in the physical landscape through time. Such a range of activities and scales requires a broad understanding on the part of the user.

These guidelines aim to help promote that understanding by examining the spread of geoarchaeological activities from different perspectives. They are intended for a range of archaeological professionals represented chiefly by curators and contractors, with the level of detail being decided by balancing the needs of those two groups. The document covers common site-forming processes, the information gained from different geoarchaeological methods, and typical on-site problems that regularly occur. Later sections offer advice on project organisation – how best to programme geoarchaeology into future projects – and how to get help once an excavation is in progress. Finally, an appendix and a glossary provide details of specialized meanings and methods.

1 Site Formation Processes and Deposits

Most geoarchaeological investigation centres on understanding how deposits were initially laid down and subsequently modified through time. The processes that played a part in the formation or transformation of a deposit are recognised by the physical and chemical properties they leave behind. In this section, the major categories of site formation process are discussed, together with any associated landforms and sediment types, where applicable. Although these categories are reviewed separately, considerable overlap may exist between them. For example, colluvium may accumulate at the toe of a hill slope on the edge of a floodplain, subsequently become reworked by fluvial action, and eventually be redeposited as alluvium elsewhere. The focus is chiefly on processes that have operated in England over the past 12,000 years, although some discussion of other periods is necessary in a few cases. Although it is difficult to make absolute distinctions, the general structure places the naturally occurring processes at the beginning of the section and anthropogenic processes towards the end.

1.1 Slope processes and colluvial deposits

Colluvial deposits (or colluvium) result from the gradual accumulation of weathered materials transported down slope by gravitational forces. The way in which they move (ie soil creep, soil flow, sheet-wash, mass-wastage) will depend on a number of factors, but is particularly influenced by the degree of water saturation of the material. Colluvial deposits occur below their source slopes and are typically poorly stratified and poorly sorted. They may accumulate to considerable depths (eg dry valley infills of several metres thickness), but may also occur on a more limited scale, where deposits build up against field boundaries such as walls or hedges to form lynchets (*see below*, Agricultural processes and deposits). Colluvium is typically a Holocene deposit and is strongly linked to accelerated soil erosion resulting from vegetation clearance, human habitation and tillage associated with arable agriculture. Solifluction deposits are another type of weathered material (sometimes called 'head') that has moved slowly down slope, induced by gravitational forces acting on saturated sediment. In Britain, the term (which simply means soil flow) is typically associated with deposits formed during the Pleistocene as a result of periglacial conditions. Solifluction deposits will form where thawing creates a water-saturated surface layer that might move over frozen subsoil; under such conditions, mass flow may occur on slope angles as low as 2°.

Key characteristics of colluvium:

- heterogeneous material, usually poorly sorted

- particle size dependent on the nature of the weathered and eroded material up slope

- bedding absent or weakly developed

- stratification poor and difficult to identify

- buried land surfaces are frequently difficult to differentiate

- often contains artefacts (pot sherds, charcoal and other material) incorporated from the pre-existing topsoil material up slope

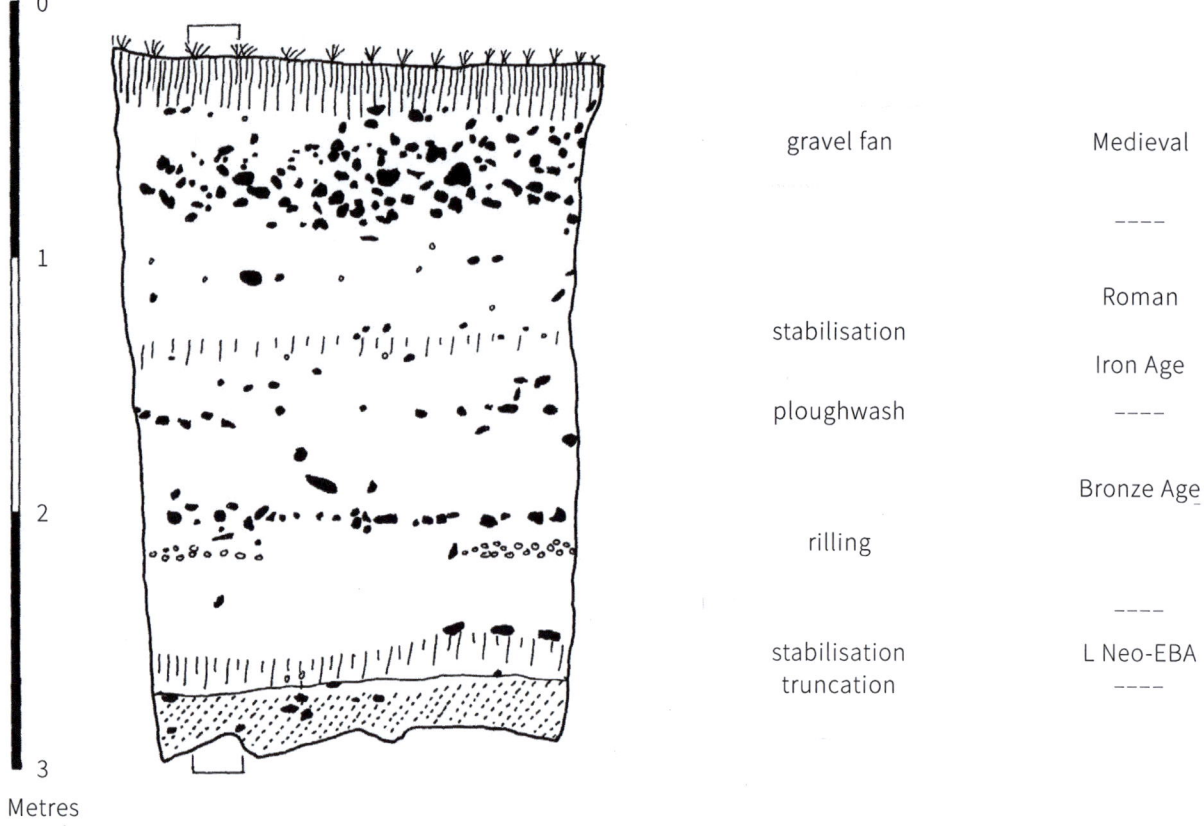

Figure 1: Colluvial sequence at Newbarn Combe, Isle of Wight
Episodes of stability are indicated by incipient soil development and thin beds of sorted stones (from Allen 1992).

Figure 2
Modern analogue for the surface erosion processes and features producing the sorted stone lines depicted in Fig 1.
© John Boardman

Colluvium normally thickens down slope and any bedding will roughly reflect the angle of the land surface at the time of deposition. Accumulation rates vary, so the depth of the deposit cannot be taken as a proxy for the time it has taken to accumulate. Relatively shallow sequences can represent long periods of time; for example a 1.5m sequence of dry valley fill, much of it colluvial, at Holywell Coombe, Kent (Preece et al 1998) represents a stratigraphic record of almost 13,000 years. In contrast, deep sequences can accumulate quite rapidly, depending on local conditions (eg almost 3m of stratigraphy at Newbarn Combe, Isle of Wight since the late Neolithic; Allen 1992).

Well-developed colluvial sequences tend to be found in dry valleys on chalk and limestone, and thus commonly display a particular set of preservation conditions. Since the sediments are calcareous, the preservation of land snails is favoured, while pollen preservation is unlikely. Pockets of (waterlogged) organic deposits that could potentially yield pollen or plant macrofossils rarely occur in the bases of dry valleys, which typically lie above the water table. Where these deposits are found, they are likely to be very localised and reflect only short episodes of vegetation cover.

However, analysis of land snail assemblages in colluvial sediments can be set against depth and used to identify palaeoecological changes through time, as the snails are deposited with the eroded topsoil from up slope and thus reflect the vegetation cover within the catchment area.

A major requirement for understanding the development of colluvium is the recognition of pauses in deposition. These stillstand episodes are represented by old land surfaces – either short-term or long-term periods of stability in which no net accumulation of deposits occurred. Old land surfaces may be indicated by subtle differences in stone content and sorting (Fig 1) probably resulting from surface erosion induced by intense rainfall when the ground surface is bare of vegetation (Fig 2). Similar surface erosion can occur at the onset of the growing season, after harvesting of arable crops, or, potentially, on overgrazed pasture.

Longer periods of stability can also be represented by the accumulation of organic matter and by soil horizon differentiation. The degree of soil development indicated in Fig 3 is unusual for Holocene sequences; here multiple buried soils are clearly defined in the dry valley sediments by the dark bands representing buried topsoil horizons. More typically, the horizons are only weakly developed and therefore differentiation of the accumulation episodes can be problematic. Detailed field description of the sequence is necessary, particularly looking for sorted stone lines and subtle changes in texture or structure. Supplementary analysis on bulk (eg calcium carbonate content, magnetic susceptibility) and oriented samples (microscopic features) may then be required to establish the degree of soil development represented (Table 1).

1.2 Alluvial processes and deposits

Alluvial deposits (or alluvium) result from processes associated with flowing water, usually but not exclusively associated with river valleys. River valleys contain numerous micro-environments (Fig 4), each of which is associated with distinctive suites of deposits that can be used to aid palaeoenvironmental reconstruction.

Alluvium is generally present as channel fills or as blanket floodplain deposits, and can be several metres thick. A wide variation in grain size is possible, depending on the energy of deposition. Upland situations support high-energy rivers, often leading to coarse alluvial deposits; lowland

Figure 3
Coastal outcrop showing multiple, alternating episodes of landscape stability (dark soil horizons) and instability (pale calcareous colluvium).

Table 1: Colluvial sequences: questions and methods of investigation		
Question	Methods of investigation	Practical requirements
Is it colluvium?	Fabric analysis of deposit to establish degree of sorting Establish degree of Stratification and relationship With local slope conditions	Field visit and description of deposit in section
Does the sequence represent a single or multiple episodes of deposition?	Analysis for recognition of old land surfaces Identification of soil development by testing carbonate, magnetic susceptibility and pedological features	Field visit and observation of *in situ* deposit in vertical section Bulk and oriented examples
How long did the sequence take to accumulate?	Absolute dating by ^{14}c rarely possible owing to nature of deposits In the absence of artefacts, two other dating techniques may be applicable: ■ OSL dating of sediments themselves may be of use in sand or silt rich deposits ■ Amino acid racemization dating may be possible on snail shells	Both techniques require samples to be taken by a dating specialist; contact regional science advisor for further details (*see below*, **Where to Get Advice**).

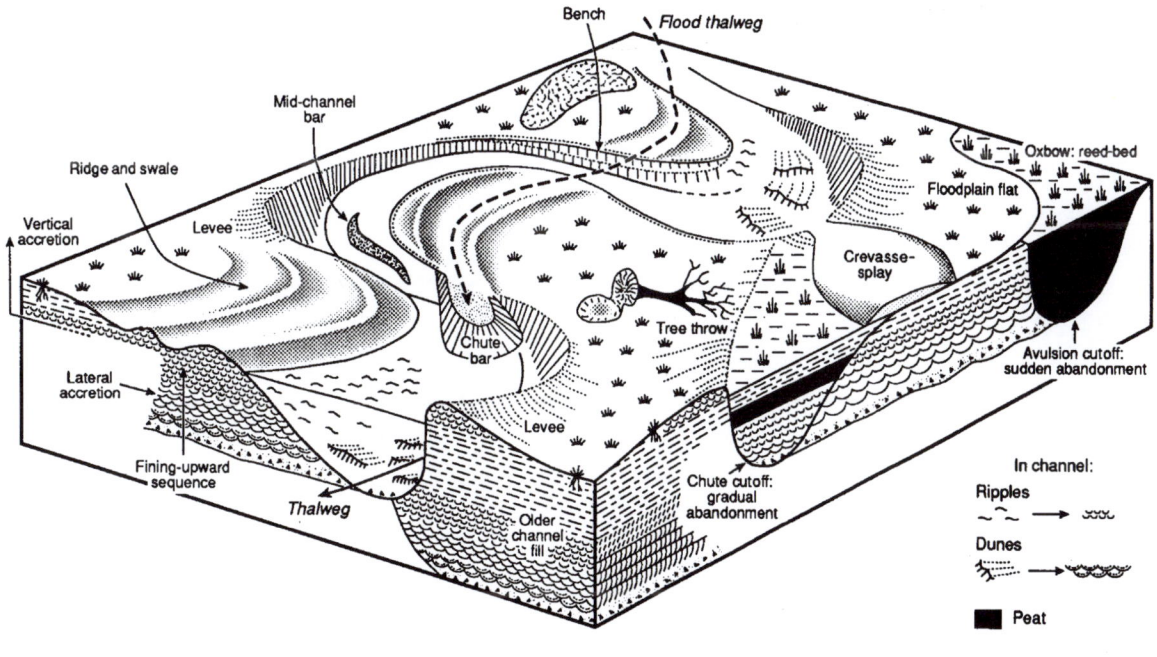

Figure 4
Diagram of river channel and associated features (from Brown 1997).

rivers are typically slower, and finer materials are able to settle out. A large proportion of excavated alluvium is waterlogged, ensuring good preservation of environmental materials (Fig 5).

Floodplains are not stable environments: they are either being aggraded (deposited) or incised (eroded). Typically, both deposition and erosion will be taking place at different positions within the floodplain at any one time. One of the effects of this is the formation of stepped river terraces, each representing an old floodplain that has been downcut. Therefore, the oldest terraces are located at higher elevations with the youngest closer to the valley floor (Fig 6). The recutting process produces parallel sequences on either side of the valley, but these are often destroyed by channel migration and reworking.

In general, terraces are composed mainly of gravels and tend to have formed during the extreme climatic fluctuations of the Pleistocene. The sequences can be used to reconstruct river movements, and ecological histories can be obtained from associated organic deposits. Gravel terraces often contain redeposited Lower and Middle Palaeolithic artefacts and can be correlated across landscapes to assist in dating elsewhere, such as in the onshore-offshore sequences in the Hampshire basin and the Solent (Bridgland 2001).

Key characteristics of alluvium:

- no diagnostic particle size as deposition depends on the energy of the water transport

- will often oxidise and change colour following exposure

- frequently laminated or exhibiting bedding structures

- may be rich in environmental evidence such as molluscs or pollen

As well as the deposits themselves, alluvial processes leave behind specific features in the landscape, knowledge of which assists with selection of sampling locations. The main feature types are:

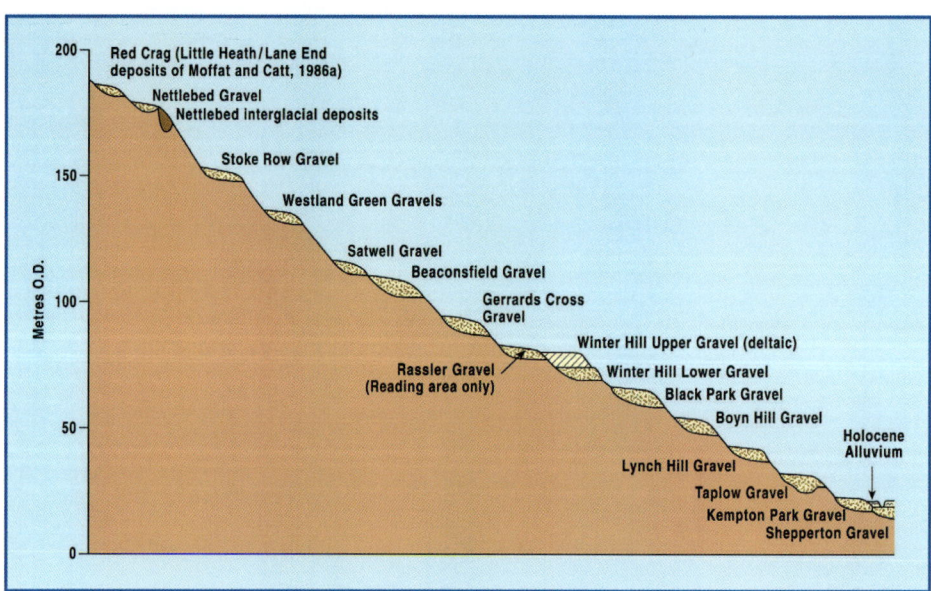

Figure 5 (left)
Alluvium often leads to exceptionally good preservation of organic materials, as in the case of this Bronze Age platform in East London.

Figure 6 (right)
Terrace formation from the Middle Thames (modified from Bridgland 1994).

In-channel features, such as islands and bars. These are formed where reduced flow rates promote sediment deposition in specific areas within a channel, ie point bars forming in convex bends, and mid-channel bars centrally located in the channel (Brown 1997, 64). The features can be used to establish information about past river regimes and the resources they offered, although they may also have been frequented for their strategic importance (eg the Eton Rowing Lake (Allen and Welsh 1996)).

Channel edge features, such as levees and crevasse splays. These are caused by overbank flooding, leading to the deposition of sediment on the floodplain in characteristic patterns. The features can bury archaeological sites – such as at Redlands Barn, Stanwick (Brown 1997, 226) – as well as show the contemporary course of the river. Additionally, braided and meandering rivers often produce relict channels and oxbow (cut off) lakes when the river abandons one course for another; these can be useful sources of environmental data.

Alluvial fans. These occur where an alluvial deposit is discharged from within a river system and spreads out, generally with a pattern of decreasing particle size from the point of origin. Again, these tend to be of interest for tracing past river routes and will also bury archaeological sites.

Archaeological significance of alluvial deposits

Alluvial deposits can be used for sediment provenancing, pollution histories and various forms of landscape study, but are particularly valuable for examining the past environments of river valleys (Fig 7). Furthermore, since these river valleys represent one of the most densely inhabited landscapes of the entire archaeological record, alluvium is likely to contain detailed information about past human settlement and cultural change (Howard and Macklin 1999). There are, however, challenges to be faced when attempting to use such data to identify the causes of river valley change, since these dynamic environments are highly responsive to both climatic variation and land-use practices. One of the most valuable characteristics of alluvium is simply its role as a preservation medium.

As rivers change course or water levels rise, alluvial deposits sometimes bury entire sites and ancient land surfaces, enabling the tracking of buried surfaces with recovery of artefactual and ecological information on a large scale. However, this can be under several metres of material (*see* Knight and Howard 1995), leading to considerable practical difficulties. The depth of alluvium can, for example, reduce the efficacy of geophysical techniques, and archaeological discoveries are often opportunistic (Table 2).

Figure 7
An alluvial sequence from North Woolwich.

Table 2: Alluvial sequences: questions and methods of investigation			
Question	Methods of investigation	Practical requirements
When and why was the alluvium deposited?	Field description and analysis *in situ*	Vertical sections to show full stratigraphic sequence
	^{14}C datable materials likely to be preserved	Organic artefacts and ecofacts collected from well-understood stratigraphic units
	OSL possible on some mineral materials	Methodology requires OSL samples to be taken by dating specialist; contact Regional Science Advisor for further details (see below, How to Get Advice).
How long did the deposition take?	^{14}C datable materials likely to be preserved	Organic artefacts and ecofacts collected from well-understood stratigraphic units
	OSL possible on some mineral materials	Methodology requires OSL samples to be taken by dating specialist; contact Regional Science Advisor for further details (see below, Where to Get Advice).
Where was the site located in the floodplain and what was its immediate environment?	Field description and analysis of deposit *in situ*	Vertical sections (or cores where vertical sections are not possible) (see Campbell *et al* 2011 for details)
	Other environmental analyses are likely to be required (eg pollen or beetles)	
How was the alluviation related to the period of human use?	Field description and analysis of deposit *in situ*	Vertical sections (or cores where vertical sections are not possible)
How deep are the alluvial deposits? Have there been inputs of other deposit types (eg colluvium)?	Field mapping of boreholes	Coring equipment and staff to carry out descriptions

1.3 Aeolian processes and wind-blown deposits

Wind-blown deposits are most commonly associated with accumulation in periglacial conditions during the Pleistocene, although more localised erosion and deposition of sediment by wind action has occurred throughout the Holocene and continues into the present day. Pleistocene wind-blown deposits can be grouped into two broad categories according to their dominant particle size. These are, loess (silt-sized material) and coversand (sand sized material). The majority of windblown deposits are thought to have accumulated during the Devensian (last glacial period), under cold, dry and lightly vegetated conditions associated with a tundra environment.

Coversands are the remnants of ancient dune systems that formed under periglacial conditions. They occur most extensively in the southern part of the Vale of York and North Lincolnshire (around Scunthorpe); smaller areas are also found in south-west Lancashire and the Breckland of East Anglia. The most extensive deposits have often been subject to commercial sand extraction. In many areas the deposits have undergone (and continue to experience) considerable reworking through localised erosion and redeposition.

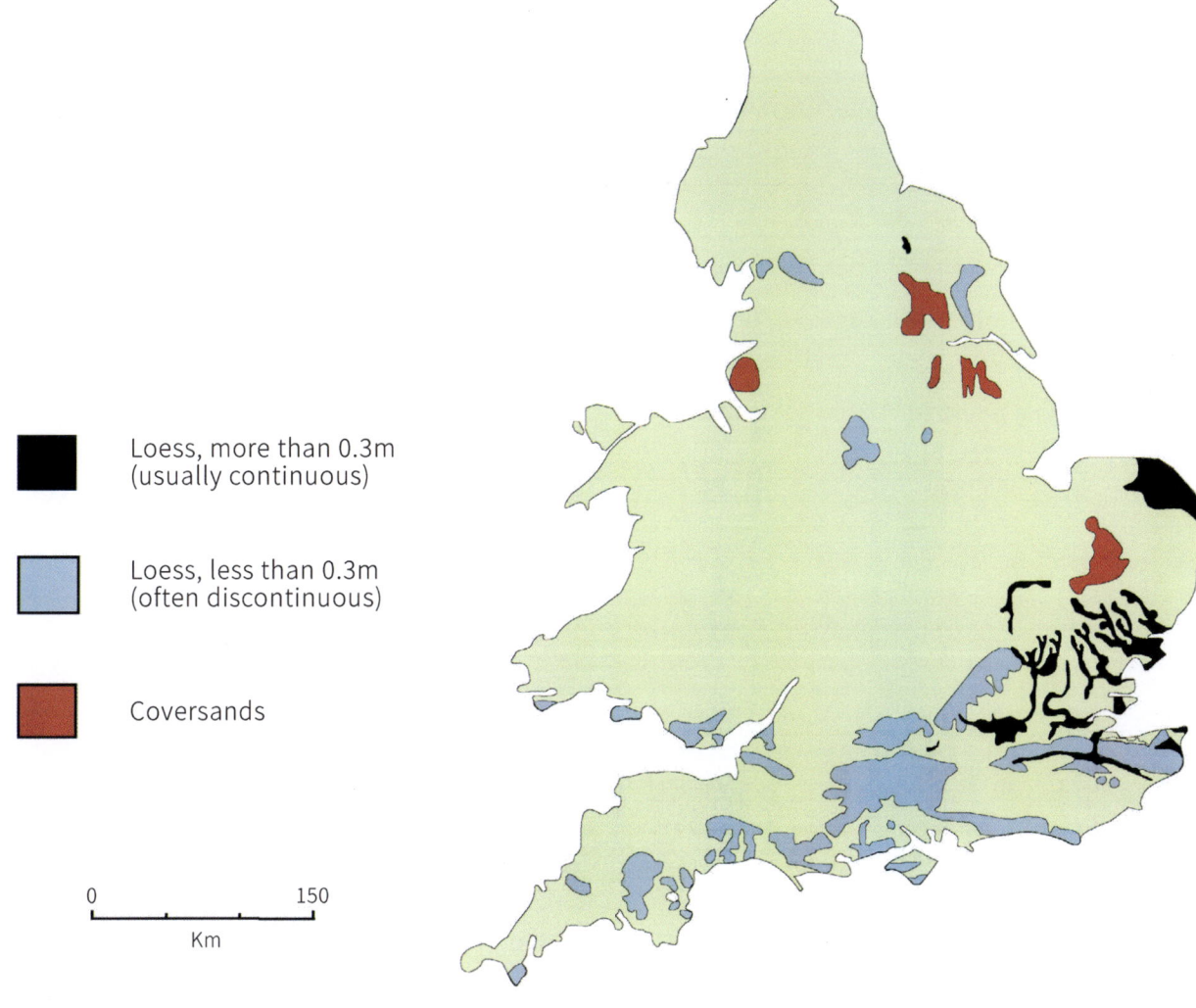

Figure 8
Distribution of wind-blown deposits in England
(adapted from Goudie and Brunsden 1994).

Key characteristics of coversands:

- predominant size is between c 63μm–2mm (sand-sized material); mean particle size is usually 100–400μm

- moderately well or well sorted (see Fig 17), although rarely as well sorted as coastal dune sand

- individual grains will be predominantly rounded to well rounded

- may have high carbonate content and contain fragments of marine shell where sediment originated from off-shore/coastal position

- material moves by saltation, and therefore tends to have moved over relatively shorter distances than the finer-grained loess

During glacial episodes, the lowering of sea level left large areas of fine-grained coastal sediments exposed while glacial deposits and outwash plains also provided a source of material that was susceptible to erosion and re-deposition by wind action. Unlike continental Europe, deposits in Britain are relatively thin and frequently show signs of reworking by cryoturbation.

Key characteristics of loess:

- predominantly 2–63μm (silt-sized material), although there may be a significant proportion of clay-sized (<2μm) material

- *in situ* deposits may have a high calcium carbonate content (as inclusions or secondary features)

- may contain distinctive heavy mineral suites, enabling correlation between individual deposits and the testing of hypotheses regarding their origin (*see below*, Mineralogy)

- particle movement in suspension, possibly over considerable distances; ie material can originate inter-regionally as it may travel hundreds or thousands of kilometres.

Both coversand and loess may subsequently be re-worked, typically by periglacial or fluvial processes. The reworking of loess by fluvial action gives rise to brickearth – wind-blown, fine textured material that has been re-sorted and deposited by water. It is typically found on old river terraces and as valley fills. Sequences containing distinct brickearth deposits are found most extensively in south-east England and correlate strongly with the distribution of the loess deposits from which they were derived (Fig 8).

Aeolian deposits (typically of sand-sized rather than of silt-sized material) have also accumulated throughout the Holocene in areas where geology, environmental conditions and land use enabled wind action to pick up and transport sediment. However, unlike the wind-blown deposits of the Pleistocene (loess and coversands), Holocene wind-blown deposits have travelled relatively short distances and are of local rather than regional significance, indicating land use rather than climatic change. In some areas, considerable depths of this Holocene material have accumulated. For example, the Anglo-Saxon site at Flixborough, Humberside, is located on wind-blown deposits that form part of the North Lincolnshire coversands, attributed to post-glacial accumulation. The site comprises nine main phases of rural settlement dating to between the early 7th and early 11th centuries AD. The latest phase of the settlement is sealed by up to 2m of undifferentiated wind-blown sand that must have been deposited during early medieval or later times (Loveluck 2007). In addition to the categories of inland wind-blown deposit described above, there are considerable areas of blown sands around the coastline of England that both seal and contain archaeological material (*see below*, Marine and coastal deposits). The major differences between inland and coastal blown sands are that the latter tend to be better sorted; their origins are linked to present (rather than past) environmental conditions; they frequently present alkaline (rather than acidic) preservation conditions owing to the fragmented shell component (Table 3).

1.4 Wetland processes and deposition

The Ramsar Convention, Article 1.1 (*see* www.ramsar.org/ris/key_ris_types.htm) defines wetlands as "areas of marsh, fen, peat land or water, whether natural or artificial, permanent or temporary, with water that is static or flowing, fresh, brackish or salt, including areas of marine water the depth of which at low tide does not exceed six metres."

Wetland deposits of various kinds are formed where these environments exist or have existed at any time in the past. As a consequence, they are commonly found in areas no longer classed as wetlands today, and often exist as interleaved deposits within alluvial sequences or under arable land. Wetland deposits comprise varying combinations of organic and mineral sediments according to the prevailing circumstances and conditions. Their main characteristic is that, being saturated with water, they contain very little oxygen. Consequently, the activity of bacteria, fungi and soil animals normally responsible for the breakdown of organic material is very low, resulting in exceptional states of preservation.

Table 3: Wind-blown deposits: questions and methods of investigation		
Question	Methods of investigation	Practical requirements
Is the sand wind-blown (as opposed to being water-lain, for example)?	Recognition and interpretation of any primary sedimentary structures present within the unit(s) Particle size analysis	Field description and analysis of deposit *in situ* by geoarchaeologist. Bulk samples of minimum 500g taken from each context in question
Is the deposit wind-blown or has it weathered *in situ* from the local geology?	Compare particle size and heavy mineral suite characteristics of the deposit(s) in question and samples of local weathered geology and /or soils	Bulk samples of each context in question, plus reference samples from local soils and underlying geology.
Does the deposit represent 'natural'?	Ensure that the deposit does not seal archaeological deposits even if it appears to be very thick (ie over 1m deep)	Auger survey (relatively rapid and cost-effective)
When and why did it start and cease to accumulate?	Stratigraphic relationships, dating and broader environmental analysis OSL dating if deposit contains enough sand that has been exposed to light in the past	Field description and analysis of deposit *in situ* by geoarchaeologist Methodology requires OSL samples to be taken by dating specialist; contact regional science advisor for further details (see below, **Where to Get Advice**) Off-site work is likely to be needed to look at local changes in vegetation cover and landuse practices (identified by pollen or land snail analysis) that may have encouraged wind-blown sedimentation patterns.

Key characteristics of wetland deposits:
- often very rich in organic material
- exceptional preservation of any organic material present, including artefacts
- very sensitive to processes promoting de-watering, increased oxygenation and increased nutrient status
- mineral deposits often grey (due to waterlogging) and have a distinctive smell

Peat is formed by plants under waterlogged conditions, when the rate of production of organic matter is greater than the rate of decay. The location of peat mires can be topographically determined, receiving water both from land drainage and from precipitation, for example in marshes, fens, flushes and carr. Mires can also develop independently of the topography, receiving water solely from precipitation, eg raised mires and blanket mires. As a result, blanket peat is commonly an upland phenomenon whereas the other mire types are typically part of lowland landscapes. The greater the rainfall, the lower the altitude that blanket peat can occur in the landscape. Topographic mires often start as lakes and may be the template from which raised and blanket mires develop. Blanket peat initiation appears also to be closely linked with human activity.

Open-water deposits are generally more diverse, comprising organic material from the plants and animals living in the water, and mineral material entering the system from watercourses and run-off. Variations of these constituents are found in the sediments from lakes, ponds, wells, canals, rivers, streams and ditches. The situation in estuarine, coastal or intertidal areas is often more complex, with interleaved deposits of varying composition formed under the rapidly changing conditions.

Archaeological significance of wetland deposits

Wetlands are archaeologically important in a number of ways. The deposits themselves, through their structure and composition, and the wide range of natural organic remains they contain (pollen, plant remains, insects, diatoms, molluscs, foraminifera, ostracods and other biological debris) can provide a detailed sequential environmental record for the period over which they formed – from tens to tens of thousands of years. Wetland deposits thus provide a landscape context for human activity. They also provide organic material well suited to dating, generally giving a reliable site chronology. Wetland sediments give, arguably, the best preserved environmental sequences of all British soil/sediment types, for example in the Humberhead Levels (Van de Noort and Ellis 1998), in the Fenlands (Waller 1994), and in the north-west wetlands (Hodgkinson et al 2000). Similarly, there can be exceptionally well preserved archaeological remains of many kinds – settlements, trackways, structures, vessels, culture layers, votive offerings, single finds and other such artefacts, within or below the deposits, eg on the Somerset and East Sussex Levels (Coles and Coles 1986; Greatorex 2003).

Locating wetland deposits and their associated archaeology

Locating wetland deposits, where their presence is not obvious at the surface, is a task for various types of coring equipment (*see below*, Coring), or could be achieved through creation of deposit models from existing geotechnical and geoarchaeological borehole logs. Locating the actual archaeological remains can be rather more problematic. Coring can again be useful, often in conjunction with various forms of remote sensing and landscape modelling. Many sites have, in the recent past, been discovered through commercial or domestic exploitation, for raw materials and fuel. Mechanised exploitation has greatly reduced the incidence of these finds (Table 4).

Table 4: Wetland deposits: questions and methods of investigation

Question	Methods of investigation	Practical requirements
How extensive are the wetland deposits?	Remote-sensing and/or coring	Air photo cover and wide ranging access for coring work
What type of deposits are they?	Coring and/or limited excavation as part of evaluation program	Field analysis of sections or cores to consider original deposition (if mineral material is present) and subsequent history of waterlogging
When were the deposits formed and how does this relate to human use?	^{14}C datable materials are likely to be preserved	Organic artefacts and ecofacts collected from well-understood stratigraphic units
	OSL possible on some mineral materials	Methodology requires OSL samples to be taken by dating specialist contact Regional Science Advisor for further details (see below, **Where to Get Advice**).
What are the characteristic burial conditions?	coring and/or excavation	*In situ* examination of sections or cores for type and degree of preservation

1.5 Marine and coastal deposits

Coastal environments in temperate climates consist mostly of cliffs with rocky platforms, beaches, dune systems or tidal flats/estuaries. Of these, rock cliffs and beach sands have low geoarchaeological potential because of the stability of the former and the extreme mobility of the latter.

Coastal dune systems can be rich in archaeology, and the sedimentary environment is of considerable significance both for the interpretation and management of the sites. Dunes often seal archaeology to great depths, but the systems can be easily destabilised, leading to erosion (eg the cists and environmental remains at Low Hauxley on the Northumberland coast (Payton and Usai 1995)). The erosion progresses rapidly, leaving the archaeological sites vulnerable both to weathering processes and to sea action. Dunes are formed from well sorted sands derived from local hard geology, drift and marine deposits. These sources have wide variations in their constituent materials and dunes will therefore show different preservation conditions correlating with geographical distribution.

Tidal files and estuarine deposits often contain deep sequences of wetland archaeology associated with silty deposits, peat layers and sometimes soil development. This evidence for the interplay of human activity, inundation and stability can be of considerable value for understanding environmental change. Areas of particular interest are the lower reaches of rivers such as the Severn, Thames and Humber, where stillstand events alternated with the accumulation of fine-grained mineral material laid down by estuarine processes. The stillstand events might represent land surfaces in a range of environments, from intertidal mudflat to reclaimed land, each having implications for the type of activities that potentially could have been supported. For example, saltmarsh that was only periodically inundated could be used for grazing and/or salt production, whereas stable land surfaces with mature soils and non-

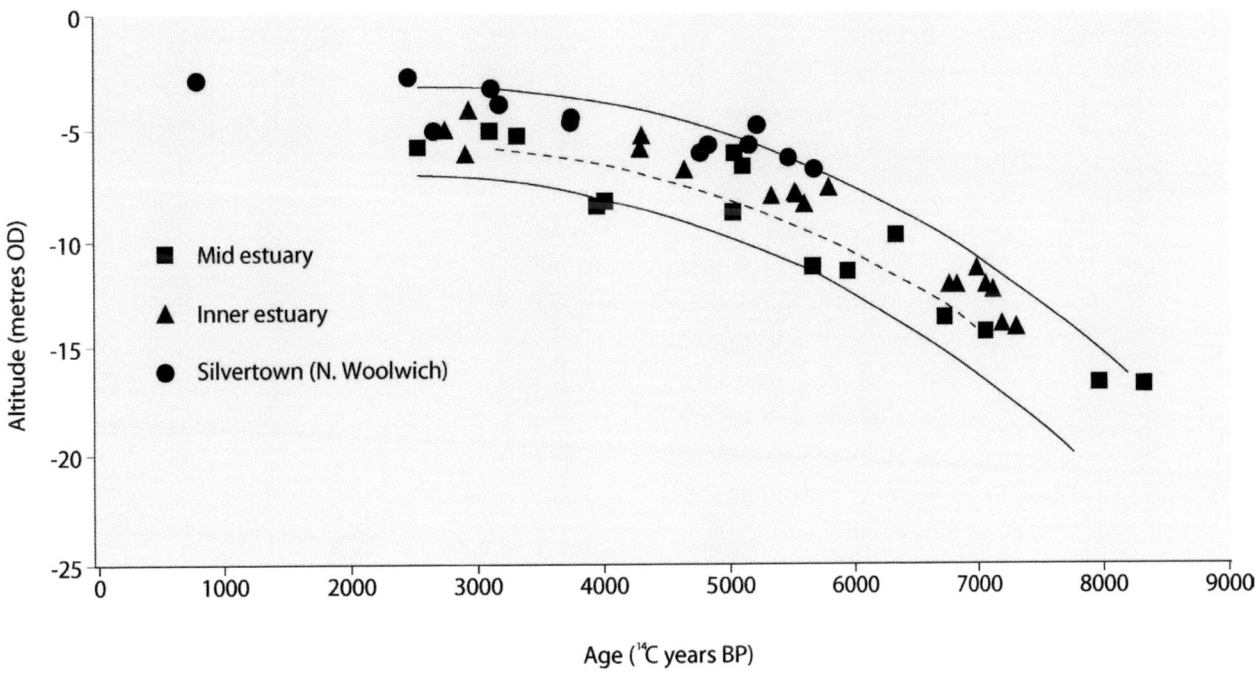

Figure 9
Relative sea level curve from the Thames estuary (from Sidell et al 2000, based on Long 1995).

saline groundwater could support arable crop cultivation. The latter is likely to indicate planned drainage systems for the purposes of deliberate land claim as seen, for example, on the Gwent Levels (Rippon 1996). Relative sea level (RSL) change may also be determined from coastal and estuarine sequences. This impinges on archaeological research in a number of areas, generally associated with land availability, navigation, spatial patterning and human adaptation to environmental change. Sea level change (relative to land) can be calculated either through modelled sea level index points, or by using archaeological structures such as waterfront quays, which can be directly related to reference water levels. These data can then be used to create a curve (Fig 9), reflecting local or regional trends. RSL change can be reflected in both organic and mineral deposits. Early models in which organic deposits simply represent regression (fall in RSL) and mineral units represent transgression (rises in RSL) have been superseded by subtler and more dynamic approaches (eg Spencer et al 1998). These recognise a range of factors and interrelationships that add greater complexity to the basic model. Organic sediment, for example, can form under conditions of rising sea level if deposition outstrips the rate of RSL rise; or significant compression might occur in a deposit, depending on the weight of overlying sediments. Care needs to be taken, therefore, when determining RSL change from intercalated sequences of peats and alluvial/estuarine muds. Deposits must be accurately dated and must incorporate materials of proven marine origin, such as diatoms and foraminifera. It is also necessary to link the deposits to a reference water level in order to integrate them with local archaeological sites. This is done through the use of modern biostratigraphic analogues; for example certain plant communities can be found forming roughly at Mean High Water of Spring Tides, while others will be found at Highest Astronomical Tide.

The coastal environment is dynamic and its changes can have significant effects further inland. Sediment movements (eg sand banks accreting through longshore drift) can rapidly change the configuration of shorelines, which can impact further up in a catchment, altering river channel dynamics and ultimately cause channel infill (eg Richborough (Hawkes 1968)). Mobile shingle spits can also seal archaeological sites, and beach ridges, once breached, can create major changes in previously stable palaeoenvironmental sequences (Table 5).

Geoarchaeology in deeper waters requires a wide range of approaches and techniques. These are currently undergoing rapid development and further information can be found in BMAPA and English Heritage (2003), Gribble and Leather (2011), Plets et al (2013) and Ransley et al (2013).

1.6 Agricultural processes and deposits

Agricultural practices have a wide variety of effects on soil. These can occur at the landscape scale, for example wind-borne soil erosion caused by clearance and tillage. Events of this magnitude are, however, difficult to distinguish from their natural counterparts. Smaller-scale effects occur more frequently and can be discerned more easily in the stratigraphic record. The most obvious process at work in all arable areas is the downslope movement of soil caused by tillage. This produces accumulations of eroded material that are often smoothly integrated into the landscape and have no obvious topographic expression. Where they are backed up against boundaries, however, the depth of colluvium (*see above*, Slope processes and colluvial deposits) becomes very apparent in the form of lynchets (Bell 1977). Another common form of erosion is by water carrying recently tilled soil rapidly downslope in rills. These are really just small ephemeral streams, and they deposit the sediment load as miniature alluvial fans where the slope angle declines (Brown 1992). As tillage actually moves soil around, even flat surfaces can develop visible topography from plough action, forming both the familiar ridge and furrow topography and also headland accumulations on the edges of fields where the plough team was turned. Ploughing deepens the topsoil in many cases, sometimes leaving plough marks formed

Table 5: Marine and coastal deposits: questions and methods of investigation		
Question	Methods of investigation	Practical requirements
How far do archaeological deposits extend under the dunes?	Borehole survey	Deep sand deposits can cause problems with some types of auger. Professional help may be needed
Was the dune system forming during the period of human use?	Field examination	Vertical sections
Has the site been eroded by dune activity?	Field examination and possibly OSL dating of sand layers	Vertical sections OSL sampling program, which has to be run by a specialist
What was the environment of deposition?	Field examination of stratigraphy in conjunction with other environmental evidence	Cores or sections for description and sampling
When was the sediment deposited and how does that relate to the period of human use?	^{14}C datable materials are likely to be preserved OSL possible on some mineral materials	organic artefacts and ecofacts collected from well-understood stratigraphic units OSL sampling program, which has to be run by a specialist
Where was sea level during the period of human use and what effect has that had?	Field examination of stratigraphy in conjunction with other environmental evidence	Cores or sections for description and sampling
Does the deposit contain any relict land surfaces?	Traces of old land surfaces may be determined through micromorphology and magnetic susceptibility	Vertical sections with suspected stillstand layers are needed for both sampling approaches
Are some context differences due to biological and chemical processes, rather than human actions?	Description and sampling across problematic boundaries for micromorphology	*In situ* samples taken from vertical sections

of darker topsoil visible in the lighter subsoil, or bringing subsoil materials to the surface. Tillage generally can promote the formation of illuvial or compacted layers (pans) in the subsoil. Preferential iron oxide deposition sometimes hardens these pans, encouraging farmers to carry out the deep, archaeologically destructive cultivation known as 'pan-busting'. Finally, agricultural activity has a wide range of chemical effects on the soil. Archaeologically, the most important was probably the addition of manure and fertilisers, which can lead to enhanced levels of phosphate and magnetic susceptibility in soils.

1.7 Wastes and construction material accumulations

Human activity inevitably produces wastes, and some of these accumulate to produce recognisable contexts or even, at some urban sites, the whole stratigraphic sequence. In general, most of the waste produced in pre-industrial societies was organic and has rotted away; but as with other organic remains, preservation can occur through reducing conditions in waterlogged contexts, or through mineralisation. This latter route is relatively common among wastes because of their high level of biological activity. Iron compounds from the soil matrix commonly impregnate organic materials, and calcium carbonate or phosphate crystals sometimes engulf or replace the original cellular structures (Carruthers 2000). Industrial societies produce a range of wastes such as slags, which are widely preserved and can provide considerable information on technological activities (Historic England 2015, English Heritage 2006).

Ash

If the organic part of plant or animal wastes is not preserved, there are still some components that are. The most common of these is ash, which is the mineral remains of the biological materials from which a fire was made. Many plants contain large amounts of calcium oxalate crystals, which are modified by heat to produce calcium carbonate aggregates. Other plants are rich in silica (phytoliths), which usually remains little changed at normal fire temperatures (Fig 11). As most fires use plant matter as fuel, ash is therefore mostly calcium carbonate and silica – the proportions depending on the type of plant burnt. Microscopic charcoal is frequently present, giving a general grey colour to the deposit. Small amounts of burnt soil, bone and vitrified slags can also be found in many cases. The calcium carbonate gives ashy stratigraphy a strongly time-dependent taphonomic character. It can remain alkaline for thousands of years as dissolution proceeds, but then rapidly acidify, producing wide variation in preservation characteristics.

At Flixborough, Humberside, this has led to exceptional bone preservation in some areas, probably where ash was thickly deposited, contrasted with other areas where bone preservation is extremely poor (Canti 1992).

Dung

Dung is rarely preserved, except in waterlogged deposits, because it is a rich food source for soil organisms. However, dung from grazing stock is often extremely rich in silica (phytoliths), from the high proportion of grasses in the herbivore diet. This can be preserved on its own, after the organic remains have decayed. Calcium carbonate is also deposited in the gut of most animals, in the form of microscopic spherulites (Fig 10). These will be preserved at neutral to high pH values and are easily recognised in micromorphological samples.

Construction materials

Human activity also leaves accumulations of geological materials that have been used for construction. In the past, earth itself was commonly used as a building material, in the form of turves, of daub (where clay was plastered onto a framework), and also of unfired clay bricks ('clay lump', 'cob' or 'clunch'). If the surface waterproofing fails, these materials all decay rapidly to form small areas potentially showing a different texture to the surrounding soils and/

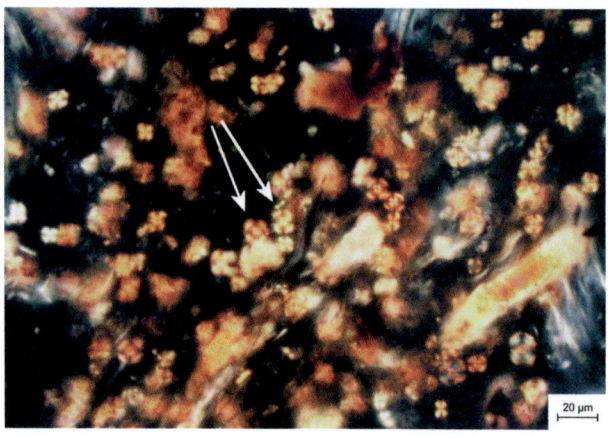

Figure 10
Thin section view of faecal spherulites in cross-polarised light (two are arrowed).

Figure 11
Ash and silica plant remains from a corn drier at Grateley, Hampshire.

or other exotic characteristics (eg inclusions of different minerals or microfossils). Similarly, mortars that have decayed out from masonry or were discarded after robbing out of walls are commonly found in soils, usually as small fragments of calcareous cement surrounding sand grains visible in thin sections. Finally, stone itself may be discarded during construction and in some cases it decays to form layers whose origin is not immediately apparent when excavated.

1.8 Soil development

Soils are the end product of a dynamic equilibrium between loose materials at the Earth's surface and the factors acting to change them. Their development involves more than simple weathering of rock or sediment. It results from complex interactions between climate, geology, topography, organisms (flora, fauna and humans) and time. Soil-forming processes become active on stable land surfaces and promote changes in the physical, chemical and biological characteristics of weathered rock or sediment (the parent material). These changes create apparent layers within the parent material, termed soil horizons, which together form a soil profile (Fig 12 and Table 6). Soil development is time-dependent and although a straightforward relationship can never be assumed, immature soils tend to be thin with weakly developed soil horizons while mature soils tend to have deeper profiles and/or well-expressed, clearly-identifiable horizons.

Figure 12
Examples of profiles from the major soil groups. Manmade soil and gley soil © Cambridge University Press; peat soil © Trent and Peak Archaeological Unit

Table 6: Soil horizon designations

Horizon	Definition	Key characteristics
O	A free draining organic horizon formed at the surface	Composed of pure organic matter. Often subdivided into L(itter), F(ermentation) and H(umus) layers, depending on degree of decomposition
H	A waterlogged organic horizon formed at the surface	Peat accumulated due to high moisture content preventing decomposition
A	A mineral horizon formed close to the ground surface	An intimate mixture of mineral grains and organic matter at various stages of decomposition and humification
E	A mineral horizon formed beneath an a, o or h horizon	Has become depleted in one or more of the soil components (eg organic matter iron or clay) owing to movement downwards through profile
B	A subsurface mineral horizon	Has become enriched in one or more of the soil components (eg organic matter iron or clay) that has moved down from overlying horizons Or has experienced *in situ* changes to modify the weathered rock/sediment characteristics
C	Unconsolidated mineral horizon	Retains evidence of rock and sediment structure and lacks the diagnostic soil characteristics of the overlying horizons
R	Consolidated, continuous hard bedrock	Solid geology

The nature of the horizons reflects the sum total of the processes at work on the parent material at a particular location. The major soil-forming processes that have acted throughout the Holocene in the UK are weathering, clay formation and clay translocation (physical downward movement of clay particles), leaching (a chemical process where rainfall encourages dissolution of certain elements and their subsequent downward percolation), podzolisation, gleying and bioturbation (*see below*, Glossary of terms). The accumulation of organic matter also plays an important role in soil development, occurring at both the ground surface from the incorporation of dead vegetation, and at depth through the incorporation of organic fragments by bioturbation and soluble material by percolation. Recognition of the processes resulting in horizon differentiation varies in difficulty. Sometimes, the nature and configuration of the horizons, as seen in the field, will indicate the dominant processes. In other situations, the processes may be less well expressed and may require laboratory analysis of the physical, chemical and mineral properties of the soil. A large number of techniques are used routinely in archaeological soil science both to assist in process recognition and to discern associated ecological conditions in the past (Limbrey 1975; French 2003). Meaningful information, however, can rarely be gained from isolated samples and almost never from samples divorced from their field context. Recognition of soils and soil forming processes begins with inspection in the field and can only be refined, not replaced, by analytical techniques.

Bioturbation

Biological activities damage archaeology in various ways. Plant roots (eg bracken rhizomes) force their way through the layers, disrupting the stratigraphy permanently, even after they die and degrade. Tree root-plates can be lifted out with soil layers attached when storms cause uprooting. Soils are also rich in animals, ranging in size from visible species such as moles and earthworms, down to microscopic mites and larvae. All of these creatures burrow into the soil for protection, and many eat it or eat parts of it. The result is a patchwork of disturbance varying in intensity according to the species involved and its population density. Burrows of the large, visible species are mostly obvious in excavations, recognizable by their shape and by the nature of the fill. One example that is not always correctly interpreted is the vertical burrows of the earthworm *Lumbricus terrestris*, which form dark stripes going down into the subsoil (Fig 13). These are often described as 'root holes', because roots will seek out the richer burrow soil and end up travelling down it, in which case the exact definition becomes academic. However, the density of these vertical stripes indicates an intensity of burrowing that is a major site formation process. These worms, along with one or two other species living more in the topsoil, destroy stratigraphic variation, bury artefacts and displace environmental remains quite extensively under some circumstances (Canti 2003).

Microscopic animals are at work in all soils. They have little effect at the larger scale, but become very significant when materials are viewed microscopically. Contexts examined in thin section are regularly found to be composed entirely of tiny faecal pellets. The process of whole soil reworking by micro-organisms usually leaves artefacts unchanged, but can be significant when the same context is being studied for microfossil work, especially pollen analysis. Both the stratigraphic integrity and the preservation conditions might have been affected, so co-sampling for soil micromorphology is recommended when pollen analysis is being carried out in paleosols (Campbell *et al* 2011).

Compaction

Compaction of soils occurs on pathways and from trampling of earth floor layers. It is characterised by an increase of the soil bulk density and a reduction of the ratio of pores to mineral matter. This diminution of the pore space is associated with a change in void shape and orientation, which may result in the formation of characteristic structures or cracking patterns, depending on soil characteristics such as particle size and organic

Figure 13
Earthworm burrows in an archaeological layer at Newark, Nottinghamshire.

matter content. On abandonment trampled areas are rapidly returned to normal porosity levels by weathering and bioturbation, but the compaction may be preserved if the layer is rapidly buried by human or natural agencies.

Effects of burning

Owing to the iron content of most soils and sediments, burning makes significant changes to their characteristics. Heating of soils above 300°C usually cause irreversible increases in the magnetic susceptibility. At the same time, heating beyond about 500°C results in a permanent change of colour towards significantly redder hues, as various hydrated or poorly crystalline iron oxides are converted to the strikingly red iron oxide haematite. However, reddening can happen at much lower temperatures, certainly as low as 350°C, and probably lower in some circumstances.

Numerous variables appear to play a part in this process, including moisture content, particle size and mineralogical characteristics. The wide range of threshold temperatures means that surface fires will not leave a visible trace at some sites, whereas at others the distinctive reddening found may not indicate particularly high temperatures (Canti and Linford 2000). Reddening is not always the result of fire, and can also occur through inherited geological colour or through some pedological processes.

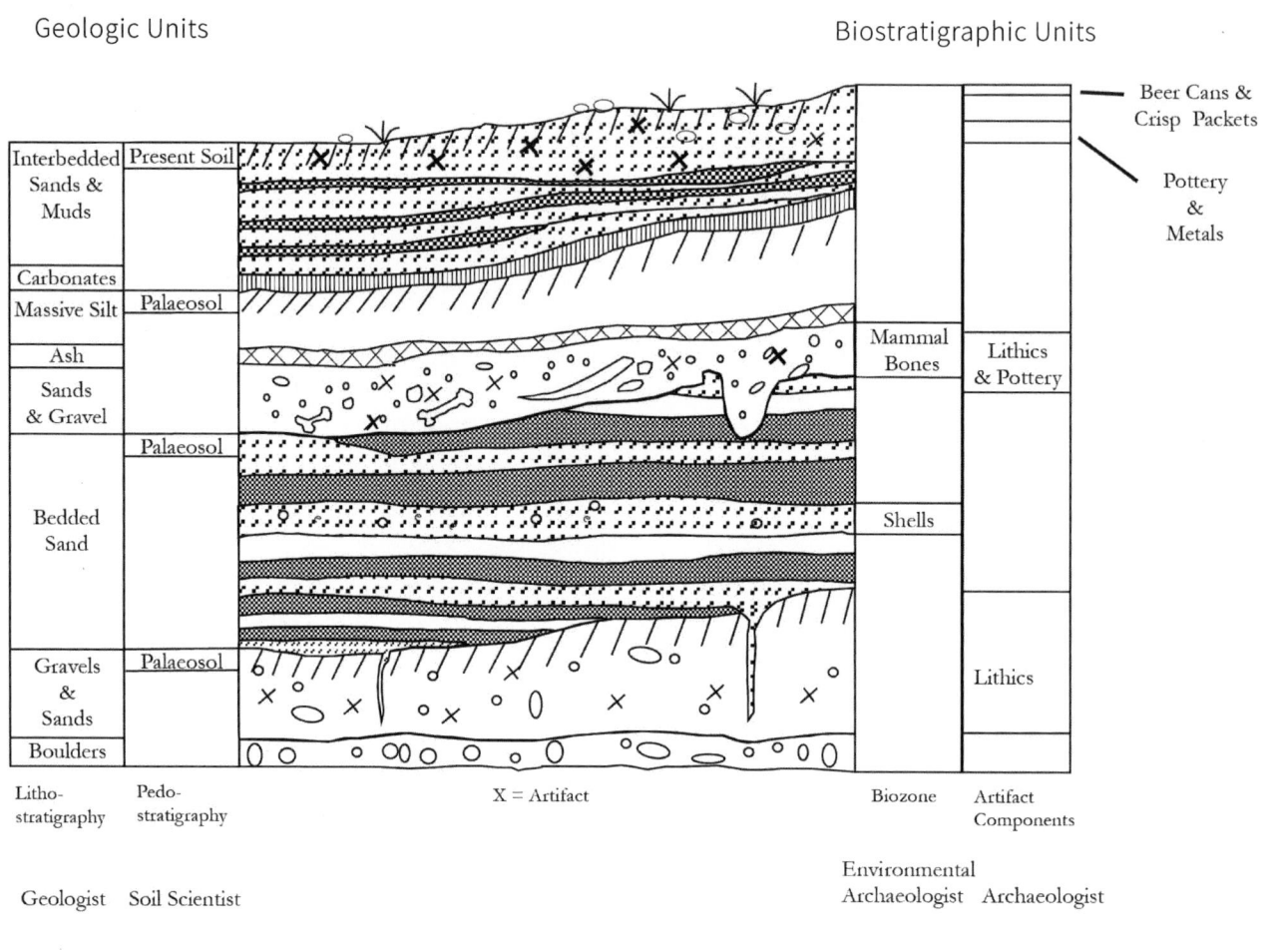

Figure 14
Variations in the interpretation of a single stratigraphic sequence (adapted from Rapp and Hill 1998).

2 Geoarchaeological Approaches to Stratigraphy

This section is intended to describe briefly the main methods used in geoarchaeology and the type of information they provide. The approaches are mostly based on established earth science techniques, and vary in the frequency with which they can be applied to archaeological situations. It is important that careful consideration is given to the archaeological questions that such methods will answer before commitment is made to the analytical costs.

2.1 Field description and interpretation

Field interpretation underpins most geoarchaeological work, and represents the single most cost-effective approach to understanding site formation processes. It may or may not be accompanied by laboratory analysis, but this must be rooted in a sound understanding of stratigraphy and the field-based development of testable ideas. In many cases, field investigations should include some study of the natural analogues for the purposes of distinguishing the human input from the purely natural processes. This can be difficult where access is limited, and even impossible in some situations (eg urban areas); in these cases, experience of the general sedimentological and pedological history of the area is valuable. The first step must be to understand the natural geomorphological processes at work in the area. This may be relatively simple and obvious to all concerned with the excavation, or it may be complex, and require dedicated fieldwork to unravel. How, for example, is the site eroding? Is there sedimentary deposition going on within the archaeological timescale, or has it all happened thousands of years previously? Bringing the information together to develop a fully comprehensive history of site formation processes requires a multifaceted approach. The same stratigraphic sequence may be recorded and interpreted in different ways according to whether it is being observed by a geologist, a soil scientist or archaeologist (Fig 14). This is because emphasis needs to be placed on different types of information in order to understand the depositional, environmental and archaeological histories of the sequence.

Additionally, the way in which individual contexts or units are grouped for interpretation may alter according to whether an understanding of sedimentary or of soil formation processes is required. Individual units can be grouped together to provide information about the changing depositional conditions, for example when multiple contexts have originally been derived from a continuous episode of fluvial activity. Alternatively, a single sedimentary unit may have become differentiated into a number of soil horizons over a prolonged period of time (*see above*, Soil development). An individual context might contain information both about how the sediment was deposited and how it has subsequently been modified by soil development. For example, Fig 15 shows a section through deposits that were laid down by water in multiple episodes under relatively slow-flowing conditions; this is indicated by the roughly horizontal primary bedding structures and by the texture of the sediment. Subsequently soil development has begun in the stable substrate, owing to the action of physical weathering and biological processes. The soil's relative immaturity can be deduced from the fact that the sediment bedding structures can still clearly be seen up to the ground surface.

2.2 Recognising depositional environments: basic descriptive criteria

Soils develop in sediments, and sediments have to be deposited by a particular process in a particular environment. Recognition of the types of depositional environment begins with examining both the individual and composite particle properties, together with any sedimentary structures exhibited by the deposit. Although further analyses may take place in the laboratory to refine the field interpretation, no amount of sampling can replace in situ examination of the deposit in the field.

Sediment structure

Sedimentary structures (or bedding) can be divided into two main categories, each of which has implications for the type of process represented (Fig 16):

Primary structures result from the way the material was initially laid down, reflecting the energy of deposition and the agent responsible, whether this was wind, water, gravity or human activity.

Figure 15
Soil development in bedded fluvial sediments (from Bridges 1997).
© Cambridge University Press

Secondary structures result from post-depositional modification of the deposits, ie they reflect processes that deformed the original deposit. Perhaps the most disruptive post-depositional processes resulting in secondary sediment structures are ice and frost action (cryoturbation) during the cold climatic episodes of the Pleistocene. In the UK, the period in which these processes are most pertinent to cultural deposits is the Palaeolithic, although recognition of cryoturbation features can always be an important part of distinguishing boundaries between natural and cultural layers. Secondary structures can also be produced by human processes, for example from loading, pit digging, tipping or other activities

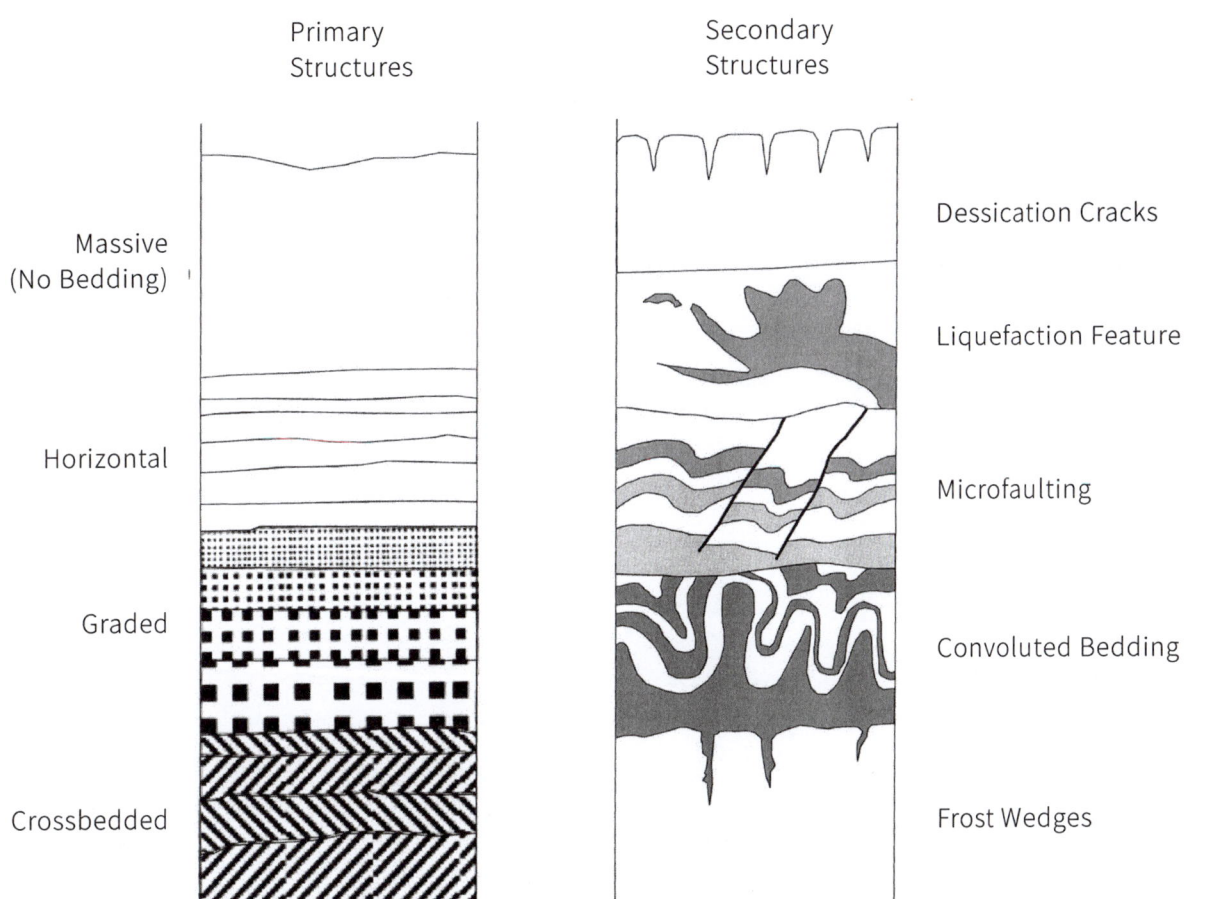

Figure 16
Primary and secondary sediment structures (after Rapp and Hill 1998).

Colour

Colour is critical in the assessment of soil processes. It indicates the state of numerous factors, such as organic matter content and iron oxidation state, which all contribute time-dependent information to site formation studies. Although tedious, formal criteria should always be used to standardise the description of colour using a Munsell colour chart or comparable method. Colour should be assessed on moist samples and away from direct sunlight (both of which can always be achieved regardless of the field conditions). Additional colour assessment may be made on dry samples but this should complement the moist assessment, not replace it. In certain environments, it can be useful to observe a depositional sequence for several hours (or even days) after it has been exposed, as weathering may pick out features that were not apparent in the freshly cleaned section. For example, the mottling effects of iron oxides may become more strongly developed, and certain minerals indicative of either the primary depositional context or post-depositional effects may become apparent for the first time, occurring as blooms on the section face (eg vivianite (blue), jarosite (yellow) or gypsum (white)). Colour changes can also occur very quickly (eg minutes) when reduced deposits are first exposed to the air.

Texture and sorting

The texture and sorting of a deposit are essential characteristics of the mineral component, needed for understanding the deposit's origin and subsequent development. Texture is a measure of the range and proportions of the particle sizes present (*see* Appendix 1 and Fig 30). Laboratory-based particle size analysis (*see* Particle size analysis) is used to formally establish the populations in an individual deposit, but a simple assessment will typically be made in the field based on finger texturing and this level of analysis is usually sufficient for descriptive purposes. Defining texture requires a classification system for different size groupings. The one developed by the Soil Survey of England and Wales, based on the definitions of the British Standards Institution is presented in Table 7, below.

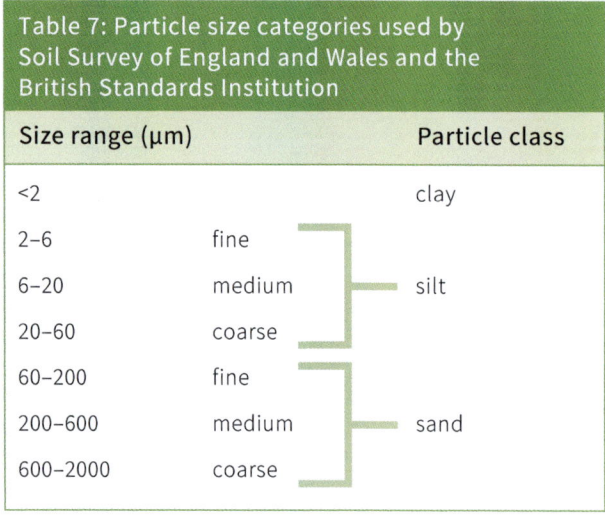

Table 7: Particle size categories used by Soil Survey of England and Wales and the British Standards Institution

Size range (µm)		Particle class
<2		clay
2–6	fine	
6–20	medium	silt
20–60	coarse	
60–200	fine	
200–600	medium	sand
600–2000	coarse	

Field examination consists of taking a small amount of the sediment/soil (a lump c 30mm diameter should suffice), moistening it, and observing closely while working it with the fingers. Coarse to fine sand grains can be observed with the naked eye; very fine sand grains and coarse silt grains may be seen using a hand lens x4 magnification).The proportion of silt and clay particles in a deposit is assessed from the workability of the material; individual clay particles can only be observed using a scanning electron microscope. Deposits with a high silt content will feel soapy and have little cohesion unless clay is also present; a pure, dry, fine silt will have the consistency of talcum powder. It should be noted that large amounts of very fine calcium carbonate (typically encountered in chalkland soils) or highly humified organic matter will tend to make the deposit feel much siltier than it really is. A full method for finger texturing

Figure 17
Three different grades of sorting in thin-sectioned sediment, ranging from A: poorly sorted (no central tendency of particle size) to B: moderately sorted, to C: well sorted material (most particles in one size grade).

is described in Appendix 1. Sorting is measure of the degree to which the particles are concentrated in one size grouping, and can provide information on the type of depositional process responsible for the deposit. An unsorted deposit will contain particles of a variety of sizes and no single fraction will dominate (eg colluvium or a midden deposit) whereas a well-sorted deposit will be dominated by one size fraction (eg a coastal sand dune). Sorting is independent of particle size; ie a well-sorted deposit may comprise anything from clay to boulders (Fig 17).

Boundary characteristics

The nature of the boundary between individual sediment units, soil horizons or contexts can provide almost as much information as the properties of the sediments themselves. A graded boundary in which one context shows a gradual transition into the overlying/underlying context indicates that there has been no truncation or erosion of the sequence and no cessation in sediment accumulation. Soil horizons also tend to show graded boundaries, although the zone over which one horizon recognisably becomes another can be as little as 5mm (Fig 18). Alternatively, a sharp boundary (ie one where a trowel point can easily be placed on the line of contact between two units) indicates one of the following: a pause in sediment accumulation, an erosive event, or a fundamental change in the nature of depositional environment (Fig 18).

Organic deposits

Organic deposits can be described in similar ways to soil materials, ie using a matrix and inclusions model, Munsell colour notation and standardized boundary types. Since they do not have a texture as such, terms such as 'fibrous' and 'well-humified' are often used in a fairly ad hoc way. This can be successful for many purposes, but lacks the element of objectivity offered by the mineral soil descriptions. The Troels-Smith system obviates this problem (Troels-Smith 1955). It is a means of sedimentary classification employed extensively within the earth science community, although rather less by geoarchaeologists or environmental archaeologists. The system was originally devised mainly for organic deposits,

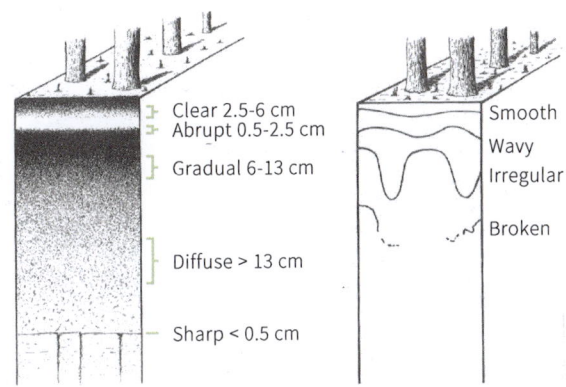

Figure 18: Boundary characteristic definitions
Measurements refer to zone of transition between units (after Hodgson 1976; drawings after Fitzpatrick 1980).

such as peat sequences; however, it is flexible enough to be used on a range of sequences including a variety of mineral deposits. Further discussion of the Troels-Smith system is in Appendix 1.

2.3 Coring

The term 'coring' covers all types of subsurface examination using mechanical devices drilled into the stratigraphy from above. It can be used in the full range of archaeological projects, from predetermination evaluation to research excavation. Coring can assist in a variety of situations to map stratigraphy (borehole surveys) and collect samples. It is mainly undertaken when the deposits of interest are too deep for conventional digging, or when large areas need to be mapped. In developer-funded evaluations, borehole surveys should not be seen as a replacement for conventional trench evaluation, but they can be used as a first phase where the results need to characterise the local sedimentary sequence and help pinpoint trench locations. Borehole surveys will need to be used in isolation in a few situations, if the deposits are too deep, or the water table is too high, for example; but basic information is better than nothing. The following sections give details of the types of equipment that can be used.

Commercial drilling rigs

Cable percussion drilling rigs are habitually used within the engineering industry to locate and characterise deposits in order to plan construction work, and the method has been adopted within archaeology to map, describe and sample certain types of stratigraphy. Additionally, many developers will make borehole logs available to archaeologists at no cost. The British Geological Survey holds a library of commercial logs that may be consulted in order to gain more information about sequences local to archaeological sites. Availability for any area can be checked at www.bgs.ac.uk/data/boreholescans/home.html. However, it is important to note that the geotechnical criteria used for the description of boreholes by drilling companies are significantly different from those used by archaeologists and geographers, so there is a limit to the value of this commercial information.

There are two ways of doing surveys using a commercial rig. First, boreholes already being drilled for geotechnical purposes can also be used by a geoarchaeologist. This approach will be the cheapest, and careful negotiation may go some way toward reconciling the differing needs of the project and the development. However, in the end, the boreholes are predominantly going to be located according to the needs of the developer rather than those of the archaeologist. Second, boreholes can be drilled for archaeological purposes in specified locations. If the developer is using a rig on site then it may be possible to negotiate use of that rig, but if not, then equipment will need to be brought in with obvious cost implications. Professional drillers can be employed to undertake the work and collect samples (Fig 19). In these circumstances, it is essential to have an archaeologist present (ideally a geoarchaeologist) noting the depths of the deposits and also ensuring that samples are collected and labelled to an archaeological standard, ie sample number, depth and, importantly, which way up the sample is. The archaeologist should also ensure that all borehole locations are surveyed and levelled in to OD.

A number of different commercial drilling rigs are now commonly used. In general they have very good sample recovery and speed, but they have to be tracked or towed onto site, and can be expensive (Table 8). Most commercial drilling rigs produce plastic sleeved samples.

Power auger

Power augers (hand-held percussion hammers) use an engine to drive various metal probes and sampling devices into the ground (Canti and Meddens 1998). They are used chiefly for logging sequences and collecting samples, usually in situations where it is impractical or too expensive to bring a commercial drilling rig onto site or where the deposits are shallower, and a rig is unnecessary. Power augers have the advantage that continuous samples can be collected with no break between them (Fig 20). However, the holes are not sleeved, which can lead to contamination, and they cannot go as deep as drilling rigs.

Figure 19
A commercial rig taking geoarchaeological cores at the Old Magistrate's Court in Bristol.
© Keith Wilkinson

Table 8: Advantages and disadvantages of various drilling methods		
Drill type	Advantages	Disadvantages
Commercial rig	■ Depth penetration ■ Sleeved holes ■ Intact sample recovery	■ High cost ■ 50-150mm loss of sediment between samples ■ Depth measurements can be imprecise
Power auger	■ Portable ■ Continual sampling ability ■ Relatively cheap	■ Unsleeved holes ■ Relatively unwieldly
Hand auger	■ Portable ■ Quick ■ Cheap	■ Relatively shallow penetration ■ Difficult to collect intact samples ■ Attrition rate on equipment

Although it is possible in some cases, a power auger will not ideally be used for deposits more than 10m deep.

Hand auger

As with the other systems, hand augers can be used for both palaeoenvironmental sampling (see Campbell *et al* 2011) and for sedimentary mapping. In this latter case, the type of auger generally used has a gouge attachment (Fig 21), which is pushed into the ground (usually a metre at a time) then pulled up and the sediment logged, before emptying ready for the next metre. This procedure is then repeated until the desired depth is reached. Owing to the relative flexibility of hand augers, it is not advisable under most conditions to use them for depths more than 6m unless sediments are very soft.

Figure 20
Power augering at Bramber Castle.
© Quaternary Scientific (QUEST)

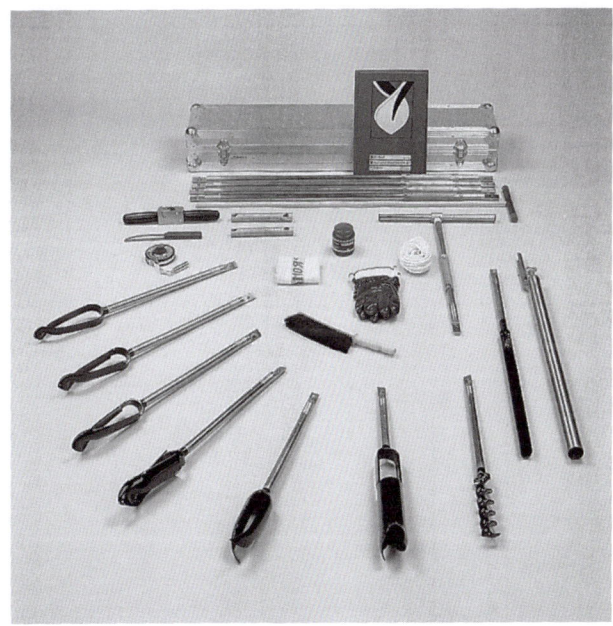

Figure 21
Hand auger with gouge head (second from right) and (from right to left) a screw head (suitable for dense soils and sediments), two heads for stony soils, and four heads for general use on fine soils and sediments.
© Van Walt Ltd

Sampling intervals

As with other types of areal survey, the correct spacing of boreholes is critical to the development of a full understanding of unseen stratigraphy. At the same time, it must be clearly stated that there is no absolute rule for how far apart boreholes should be, and some experience can be needed to get it right. Most obviously, the successful finding of any structure or object can only be guaranteed by placing boreholes closer together than the object's minimum dimensions. This could be expensive if carried out too rigidly, and strategies for avoiding unnecessary work are usually apparent on the ground. Where boreholes are aimed at examining stratigraphic change for example, costs can be minimised by spacing the first holes far apart, predicting the intervening stratigraphy, then testing that hypothesis with further judgemental boreholes between the preliminary ones.

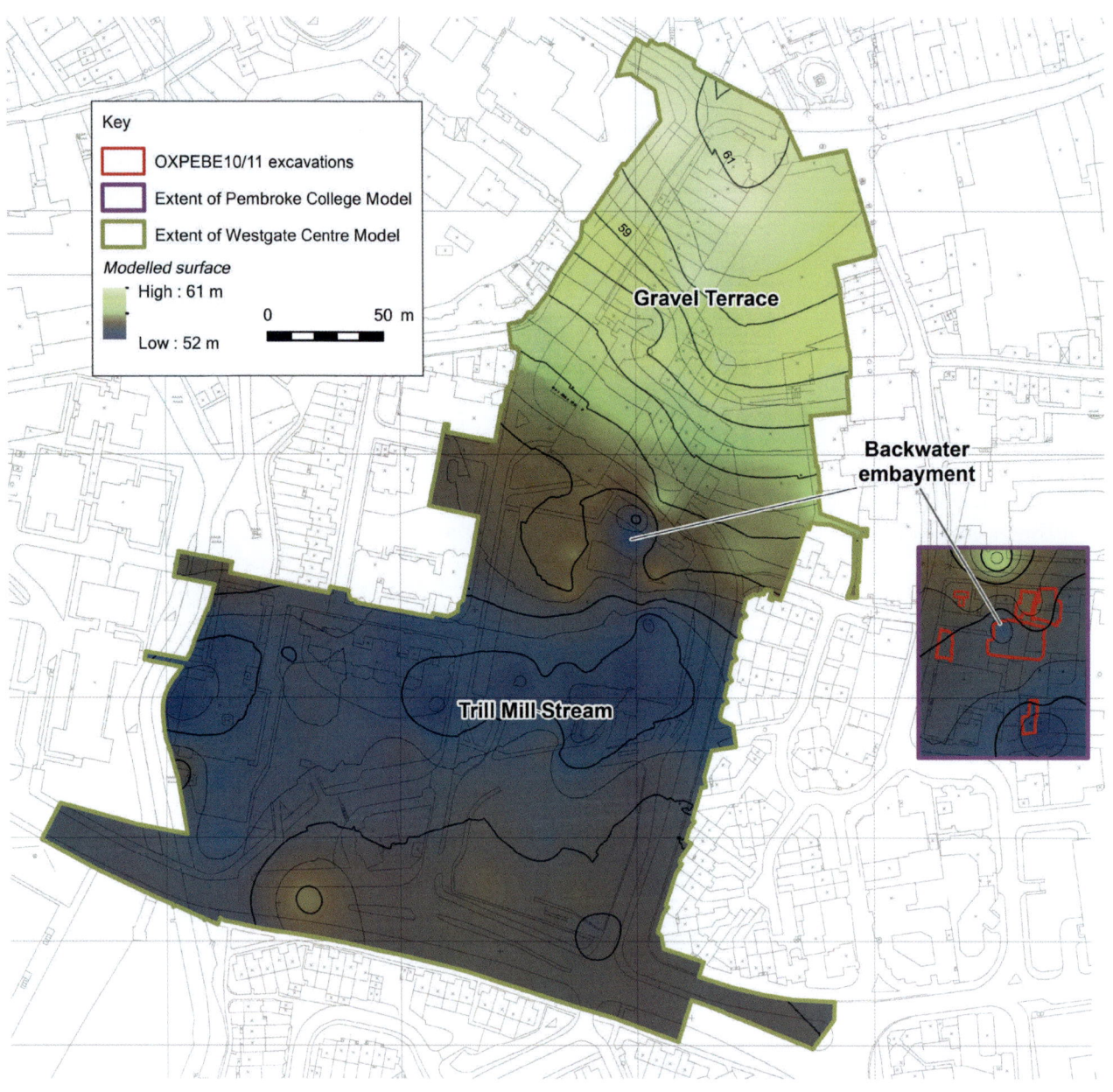

Figure 22a
Pleistocene gravel surface topography.
© Oxford Archaeology

Reporting

Once the survey has been completed, a report should be prepared addressing the research issues highlighted in the brief, specification or written scheme of investigation agreed for the project. Some sort of cross section will always need to be drawn, and topographic models generated from grid surveys can also be useful (Fig 22; *see also* Bates and Bates 2000; examples can be found in Bates and Stafford 2013, Corcoran *et al* 2011 and Swift 2007). A range of software is available for undertaking this type of modelling, from straightforward CAD packages, through models produced entirely in GIS software, to complex packages such as RockWorks (Rockware Inc). If trench locations are being suggested on the basis of the results, these should also be shown on the figures.

2.4 Soil phosphorus analysis

Phosphorus pervades all ecosystems as compounds in plant and animal tissues and in a wide range of inorganic and organic forms within the soil. Phosphorus is constantly recycled from organisms (plant and animal) to soil and back again, although only a small proportion of the total phosphorus present within the soil environment will be actively involved at any one time. In addition to this background recycling (occurring without human intervention), phosphorus can be introduced into settlement areas from excreta (human and animal), the burial of corpses and carcasses, organic building materials, refuse and food processing or storage. Archaeological soil phosphorus analysis is employed on the principle that human activity acts to redistribute phosphorus, increasing the levels in some areas through concentrated deposition of organic materials or decreasing the levels where, for example, arable cultivation and harvesting without manuring is practised. The reason that these activities are potentially detectable in the archaeological record is that phosphorus becomes fixed rapidly on deposition in most soil types, is relatively stable compared to other

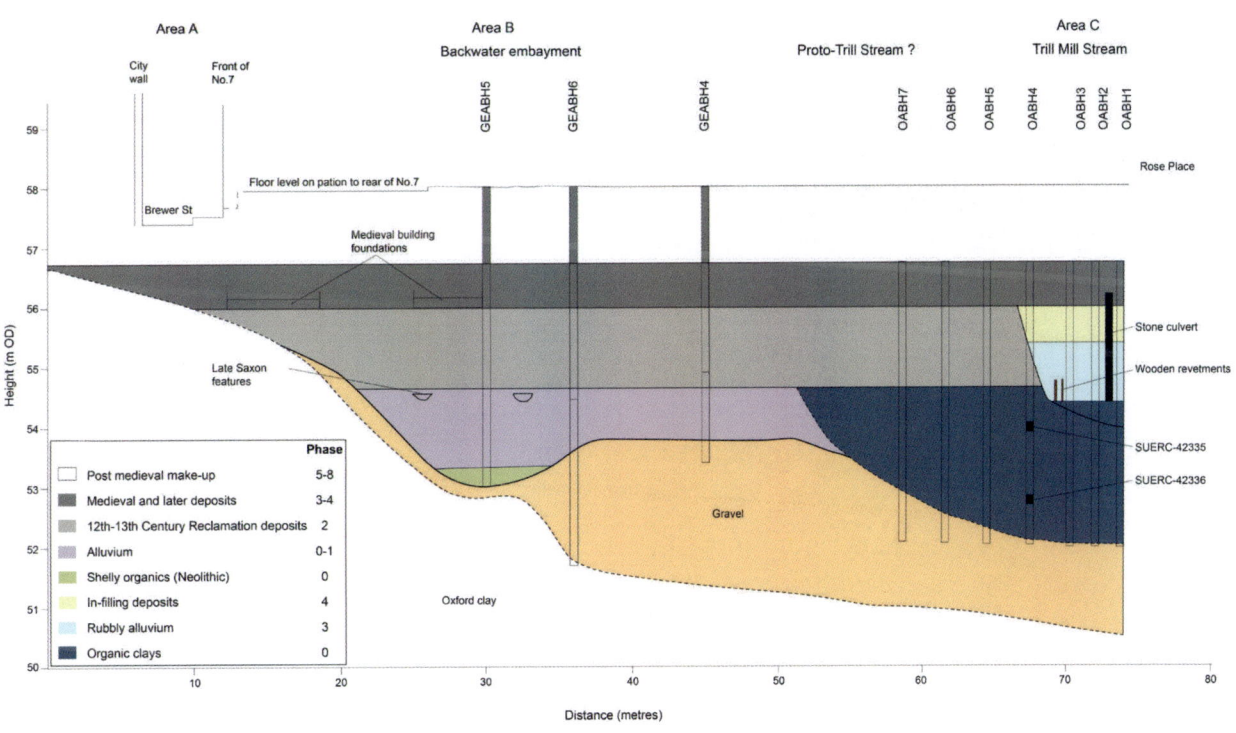

Figure 22b
Interpretative borehole profile of the Westgate Centre and Pembroke College, Oxford. © Oxford Archaeology

elements within the soil system and is largely resistant to leaching. The traditional applications of soil phosphorus survey can be identified as falling into one of the following categories:

- prospection and survey to identify and delimit sites

- determination of activity areas within settlements and sites

- information on past land-use practices

- interpretation of individual features and/or deposits (Conway 1983)

It should be noted that soil phosphorus analysis, particularly as a survey approach, is most successful when combined with other techniques, such as fieldwalking, borehole survey, geophysics or aerial reconnaissance. For a valuable discussion of phosphate methodology and applications, *see* Craddock *et al* (1985).

Reference samples

Difficulties in the interpretation of phosphorus surveys can arise from a number of factors unrelated to past human activities, namely:

- natural background variations in phosphorus concentration

- spatial variations in the phosphorus retention capacity of the soil

- vertical variations in phosphorus within soil profiles

- effects of recent phosphate inputs from fertilizers, manure, grazing animals or other sources

With respect to the last point, the relationship between modern land-use practices and archaeological soil phosphorus concentrations is poorly understood. In particular, research is needed to assess the degree to which modern fertiliser inputs could affect the concentrations of both available and total phosphorus in underlying archaeological layers. Simple procedures are already in use to limit the effects of the first three factors identified above. Taking them in turn, the influence of naturally occurring anomalies (both high and low readings) can be reduced by taking reference samples to measure the natural background variation on a site-by-site basis. These values will automatically be included by chance sampling in large-scale prospection surveys. However, in the more targeted type of phosphate work in restricted areas, where features are sampled to aid interpretation of their function, separate reference samples will be required from an area lying outside the feature(s) of interest. This applies regardless of the size of feature being studied, ie it is applicable to fields, enclosures, floors within structures or fills. Reference samples are crucial for understanding soil phosphorus data, as individual concentrations (eg 2500ppm) have no inherent interpretative value and can only be understood in comparison to the surrounding concentrations. It is not always possible to limit the interpretative problems created by the phosphorus retention variability and the variable distribution with depth through the soil profile. The retention capacity is largely determined by soil texture and pH, so the most secure interpretations of genuinely enhanced levels created through human activity (rather than through natural variability) will be made on samples from deposits with comparable values for these characteristics. Although the vertical distribution of phosphorus through the soil profile can be complex, overall there is a tendency for a marked decrease in concentration with depth (Fig 23). Wherever possible, therefore, reference samples should be taken from material of comparable texture and depth to the area being studied; deviation from these ideals can result in spurious distribution patterns.

Sampling intervals and sample size

Phosphorus surveys are usually conducted on a grid system, the sample intervals being determined by the size of the area of interest: typically between 1m and 20m across sites and 0.2m and 0.5m within individual structures, with the precise intervals being clearly dependent on the nature of the information sought. A less

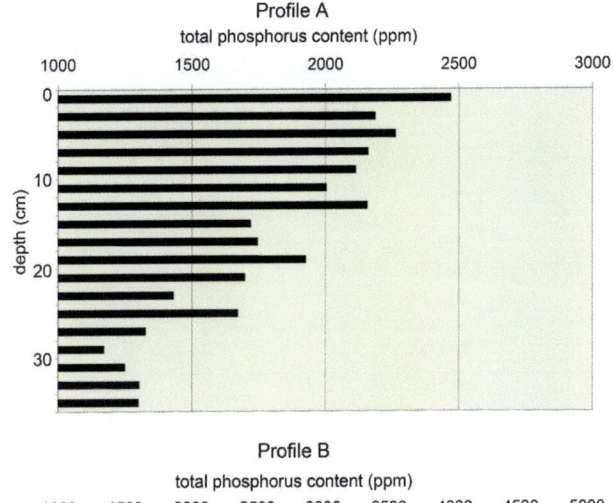

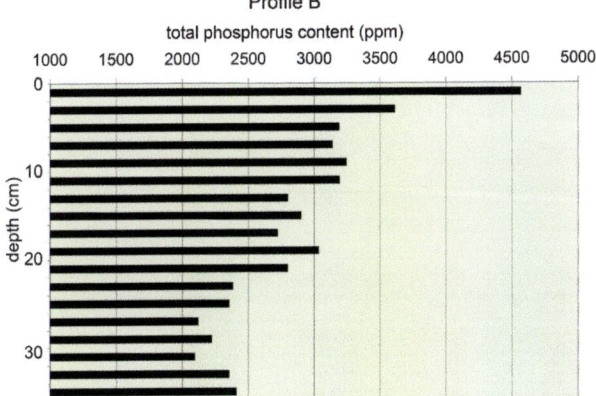

common approach, but one that can be very effective, is radial survey. Here, transects radiate out from a focal point of known archaeological significance with samples taken at regular intervals along each line (Fig 24). This style of survey may be of particular use to delimit the zone of activity associated with, for example, an individual feature.

It should be recognised that quantitative analysis for phosphorus (and other elements) is relatively costly per sample (consult Science Advisor for current costs). Considerable time should therefore be spent deciding on the minimum number of samples necessary to yield the kinds of data that will allow interpretative statements to be made. This process can be desk-based but should include the site director and/or supervisors and the specialist approached to conduct the analysis. Scaling down the size of the survey and the sample set is often not a sensible option, and it may well be better to re-evaluate the reasons for the survey and abandon

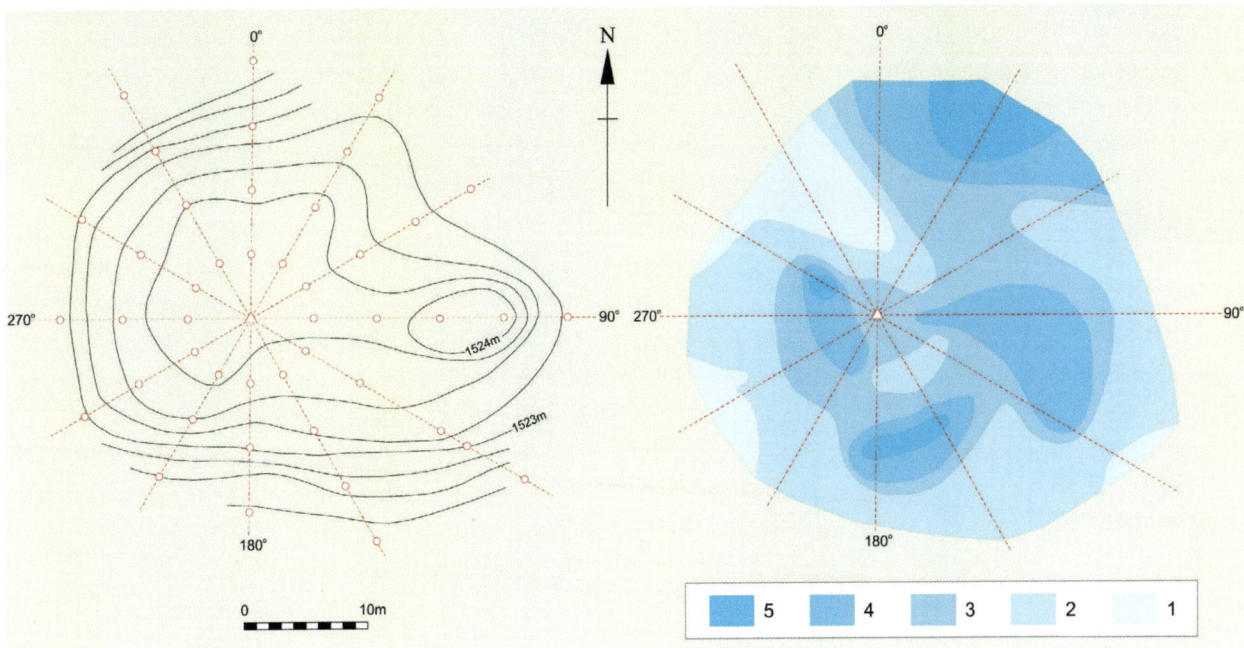

Figure 23 (above top)
Distribution of total phosphorus through two soil profiles, showing typical variability and overall trend of decreasing concentrations with depth.

Figure 24 (above)
Radial survey conducted to delimit archaeological activity; the isolines were drawn to identify areas with significantly enhanced levels of phosphorus and used to position evaluation trenches (after **Lippi 1988**).

it altogether if financial constraints prevent the taking of the minimum number of samples.

Analytical methods

A number of methods can be used to assess the concentration of phosphorus present in soil samples and these vary in the type of phosphorus fraction (available, organic, inorganic or total phosphorus) detected. Most rely on the extraction of a proportion of the phosphorus using acids or alkalis with, or without additional reagents. The amount of phosphorus in the resulting solution is measured by introducing other reagents that form a complex with the phosphate ions and then develop colour, the intensity of which is proportional to the amount of phosphorus present. The intensity of the colour can be assessed visually (as in the spot-test) or accurately measured by a colorimeter or spectrophotometer (eg for total phosphorus analysis). A summary of the advantages and disadvantages of the most commonly used methods is presented in Table 9.

Outline methods for the analyses presented in Table 9 can be found in Gurney (1985), together with references that can be consulted for the full protocol, equipment and chemical requirements for each analytical technique. However, details of the spot-test (alternatively known as the Gundlach method or ringtest) are provided in Appendix 1 for ease of reference.

2.5 Multi-element geochemical analysis

The elemental composition of soil is influenced predominantly by the nature of the geological materials in which it has developed. However, human activities associated with agricultural, settlement and industrial practices may also affect the elements present, creating anomalous, localised accumulations of chemical elements in a particular locality. These anomalies are potentially identifiable in the archaeological record, as the elements can be present in compounds that are resistant to leaching.

Advances in technology for analytical chemistry have made the quantification of multiple elements from a single (small) sample practically and commercially viable for archaeological purposes. However, research on the taphonomy of individual elements is still in its infancy and, with few exceptions, their value as diagnostic indicators of anything other than generic human activity is poorly understood. Multi-element analysis employs methods capable of quantifying a number of individual elements (the number analysed varies considerably between surveys, ranging from less than 10 to more than 30 elements) but will typically include phosphorus and metals (eg lead, zinc, copper, cadmium). Analyses of other soil properties, such as organic matter (assessed by loss on ignition) and magnetic susceptibility, are often conducted in association. Theoretical and practical considerations of these additional techniques are discussed below under the relevant headings. The use of multi-element geochemical survey as a prospection technique for the identification and delimitation of archaeological sites has increased over the past decade. At Shapwick, Somerset (Aston et al 1998) nine elements (phosphorus, lead, copper, zinc, cadmium, nickel, manganese, cobalt and chromium) were quantified over an area where previous earthwork survey, geophysical survey, fieldwalking and limited excavation had showed a concentration of settlement activity dating to prehistoric, Roman and medieval periods, the last including the site of an old church. Elevated levels of phosphorus, lead (directly coincidental with the site of the church) and zinc corresponded to the focus of settlement activity identified by other means. However, the remaining elements either showed concentrations away from known archaeology (nickel, cobalt, chromium and manganese) or showed no clear pattern (cadmium and copper). Analysis of the elemental composition of soils can also be used as a tool to aid the interpretation of archaeological structures and features. This has been done infrequently and the provenance of particular elements is rarely considered from the perspective of activity type and its link to concentration (or depletion) at a particular location. One of the few British applications of this approach is presented in a study of historic land-use practices surrounding

Table 9: Comparison of the advantages and disadvantages of different methods for the detection of soil phosphorus for archaeological purposes (after Gurney 1985)

Method	What it measures	Advantages	Disadvantages
Spot test* see: Schwartz 1967 Eidt 1977	Proportion of the available phosphorus	■ Cheap, quick and easy to use ■ No sample preparation required ■ Rapid availability of results means immediate feedback to survey/excavation strategy possible ■ After brief training session can be conducted by site staff rather than specialist	■ Qualitative data ■ Results can be difficult to interpret and can be misleading ■ Easy to create artefacts in data set if strict protocol is not followed ■ Only suitable for prospection and site delimitation
Available phosphorus	Phosphorus available to plants (labile fraction)	■ Quantitative data set ■ Simple analysis ■ Data can be formally analysed ■ (By statistical methods) to identify areas with significant concentrations of soil P	■ Amount can fluctuate over short periods of time ■ Slow feedback of results as samples must be processed in laboratory – results unlikely to be available within the period of fieldwork ■ Strict protocol must be followed as even slight variations in temperature can affect the amount of soil P extracted by reagents ■ The relationship between available phosphorus and ■ Phosphorus added through archaeological activity ■ Over time is poorly understood (ie The amount of ■ Available phosphorus does not always reflect the total ■ Quantity of phosphorus present in a soil system)
Inorganic phosphorus** see: Sieveking et al 1973	Inorganic component of phosphorus	■ Relatively quick and can be adapted for use in field or laboratory ■ Minimal sample preparation (air-dry & screen) ■ Analysis relatively simple to perform ■ Yields quantitative data	
Total phosphorus	Organic plus inorganic components	■ Quantitative data set ■ Data can be formally analysed (by statistical methods) to identify areas with significant concentrations of soil P ■ All fractions of phosphorus in the soil sample are extracted and measured; therefore obviating the need to understand the relationship between available phosphorus and that incorporated through archaeological activity	■ Relatively expensive, labour intensive and with slow feedback of results as samples must be processed in laboratory regardless of protocol for conversion of organic to inorganic phosphorus and subsequent extraction/measurement methods ■ All phosphorus in the soil is extracted and measured, ncluding fractions that are not archaeologically meaningful (eg inherited from geological deposits)

*Alternative terms: Gundlach method; ring test **alternative term: Lovibond method

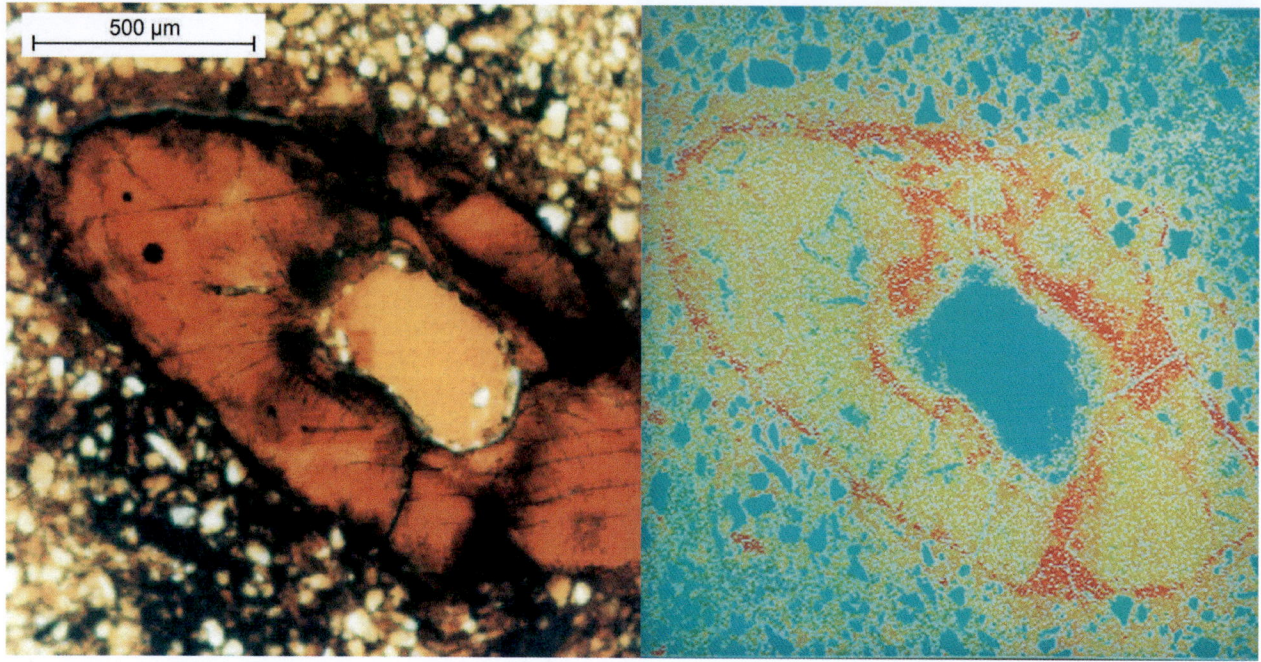

Figure 25
Elemental map of a thin section showing iron concentrations in a feature compared to the microscopic colour in cross polarised light.

---

a clachan (or farmstead) on the Isle of Skye (Entwistle and Abrahams 1998). Here, elevated levels of calcium and strontium (with respect to those of adjacent land) were thought to be caused by the application of coastal sand as a manuring material to fields used for the cultivation of arable crops. Concentrations of heavy metals and trace elements can also be used as stratigraphic markers and for the correlation of units across spatially extensive sites, particularly in fine-grained sequences deposited by fluvial or estuarine processes (Wilkinson et al 2000). They have also successfully been used to identify landscape changes resulting from the impact of mining activities in floodplain sediments (eg Taylor and Macklin 1997) and associated pollution (Hudson-Edwards et al 1999).

2.6 Micromorphology

Micromorphology is a technique that allows the observation of undisturbed soil and sediment samples at various magnifications with instantaneous recognition of most constituent materials. Whole intact blocks of sediment or soil are removed from the stratigraphy and impregnated with resin. A slice is then cut from the block and ground to a standard thickness of 30μm. The manufacturing procedure takes time (usually some months), so it must be planned for when projects require rapid turn around of results. The thin section can be used for close examination of a wide range of questions presented by the stratigraphy (Davidson and Simpson 2001). This is typically carried out on a petrological microscope with various controlled light sources. Both thin sections and impregnated blocks can also be examined using an electron microscope, which can resolve particles to submicron sizes (less than 0.001mm). If this is accompanied by use of a microprobe, it is also possible to get a full elemental analysis of material contained in tiny areas of the thin section (Fig 25).

Whatever the approach, answerable questions are typically those where microscopic differences have a definable link to site formation processes. For example, Heathcote (2000) was able to determine whether there were depositional stillstands and soil development phases within alluvial sequences in the Somerset Levels by comparison of the microfabric types, weathering state and organic matter of the layers in thin section. Micromorphology is well suited to comparisons of deposits with parent materials and this approach represents another fruitful area of study at some sites. Deep 'garden soils' are regularly found in St Andrews, Scotland and have been generally interpreted as material deliberately imported for horticultural purposes. Carter (2001) showed that the microfabrics consisted of about 20% fuel residues, domestic waste and building materials. The remaining 80% was similar to the local soil materials but could have been imported as turf or daub for construction purposes, with bioturbation accounting for the mixing and destruction of any detailed stratigraphy. This result has close similarities to the interpretation of the so-called 'dark-earth' deposits in London, put forward by Courty *et al* (1989). Inclusions of microscopic wastes are also an important component of micromorphological studies into the use of domestic space. Simpson *et al* (1999) examined thin sections to identify a preliminary occupation phase and a subsequent waste dumping phase for the great pit at Hofstadir, Iceland. Evidence for the former included a sedimentary microstructure of horizontal planar voids and vesicles, while the latter was indicated by various wastes including ash, food remains and charcoal. Larger-scale issues, such as soil and landscape histories, can be enhanced significantly by micromorphological analyses. In these types of study, micromorphology will tend to be complementing a range of other approaches to help build up a large-scale picture of environmental change (eg French 2003, Chapter 12). In some cases, thin sections may need to be described using standard methods and parameters. The results formalise the microscopic view, enabling comparisons to be made of the nature, relationships and history of many mineral and organic components (Fig 26). However, the descriptions should be seen as tools of analysis rather than as analyses in themselves. Micromorphology needs to be done for a purpose, and both the question it addresses and the type of answer that is expected should be very clear to the excavator and project manager before the expense of manufacture and analysis is incurred. The extraordinary potential of this technique is matched closely by the inherent difficulties of communication it presents. Non-specialists find it hard to form a view on what can be determined, and are generally unable to make a technical judgement when presented with results. This puts an additional onus on the specialist to provide clear explanations of what it all means. Detailed micromorphological descriptions, where needed, should be presented separately to avoid overburdening the central aims of the work. It is important that the archaeological reasoning and a jargon-free account of the supporting microscopic evidence form the bulk of the report.

2.7 X-radiography

Blocks of soil or sediment can also be subjected to x-ray photography (x-radiography) to yield information not immediately visible to the naked eye. X-radiography of sedimentary materials highlights areas of greater or lesser density, due either to differences in the constituent materials (eg slight textural changes) or to variations of their compactness. Thus, iron mottling will show up as light patches on the radiograph, and a compact

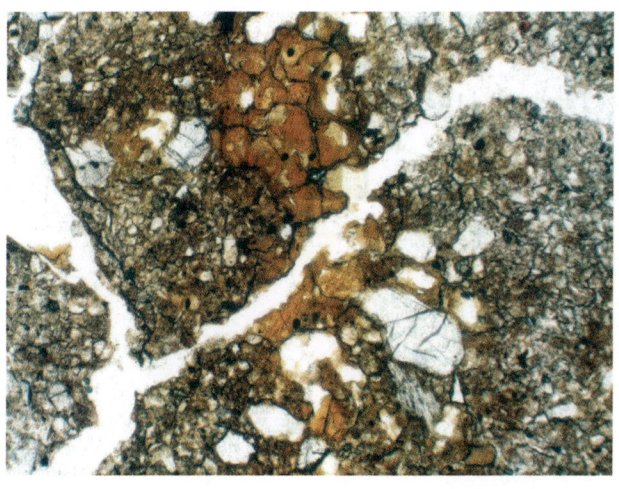

Figure 26
Thin section view of waterlogging features (gleying) from below the surface of an animal stabling layer.

layer of clay in a coarser sedimentary sequence will produce a thin pale band. This visual similarity makes interpretation more difficult than for thin sections, but the results can yield insights into important sedimentary and post-depositional processes. They can assist, for example, with interpretation of biostratigraphic results, by clearly showing zones of disturbance. In general, situations where context definition is hampered by similarity of materials or colour (eg alluvial sequences) may benefit from x-radiography, but its use must be based on an answerable need rather than simply hoping something will turn up.

2.8 Mineralogy

Except in peaty situations, most stratigraphy consists of a mixture of organic and mineral materials. The mineral component is largely quartz (particularly the silt and sand sized grains) or clays, with additional feldspars and calcium carbonate in some places. Small percentages of other minerals are always present, however, and these can be significant depending on geographical area. Minerals such as zircon, tourmaline and garnet are found everywhere in the soil as a result of their extreme resistance to weathering. Less resistant varieties such as chlorite and hornblende are often present as well, and can be sensitive indicators of source area. Together, these are known as 'heavy minerals' because they are heavier than quartz – a property exploited in the laboratory to separate them off. The heavy minerals can be identified under the polarising microscope and counts produced to show different trends in origin. The technique is therefore valuable for provenancing of sediments, building materials or wastes in any geographical area where the source rocks show significant variation (eg Catt 1999). In addition, wind-blown material, coming from long distances, can have distinct mineralogical differences when compared to underlying material. Minerals also grow in some stratigraphic situations as a result of biological processes (biomineralisation). Vivianite and various forms of calcium phosphate, for example, will often replace organic materials or crystallise in the spaces between them (Fig 27).

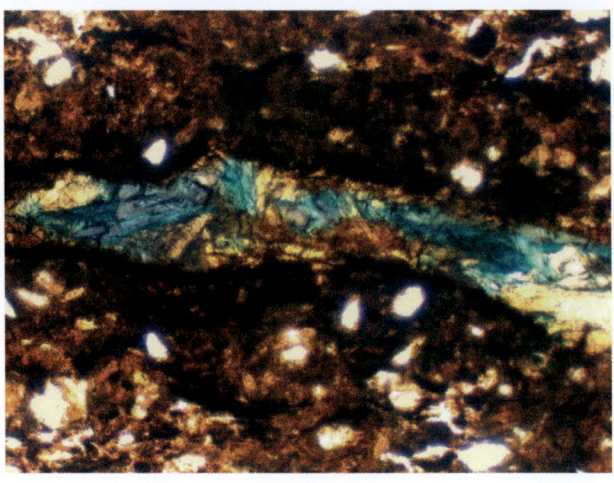

Figure 27
Vivianite crystals (blue and green) growing between layers in the turf stack of Silbury Hill.

Calcium carbonate precipitates through bacterial action as very fine needles in some soils and is actually produced in granular form by special glands in earthworms. Tiny spherulites of calcium carbonate are also produced copiously in the gut of some herbivores, and these can end up forming a significant component of layers containing dung (*see* Fig 10). Plants produce silica (phytoliths) which is preserved in most soils, providing evidence for previous vegetation and addition of plant materials.

2.9 Particle size analysis

Particle size analysis is the laboratory equivalent of finger texturing (*see above*, Field description and interpretation), and provides an accurate breakdown of all the grain sizes. It is carried out using analytical sieves for the coarse end of the particle-size spectrum (sand size or larger) and various sedimentation or diffraction-based systems to test the silt and clay. The particle size distributions reflect the textural characteristics of the original geological source material, the changes arising from any depositional processes, and, in some cases, post-depositional effects and soil formation. Particle size analysis is therefore valuable for looking at sediment source areas, and some aspects of sedimentary or pedological processes, such as sorting and clay translocation. Particle-size has suffered, like many geoarchaeological techniques, from over-use in situations where it is not really needed. The tests are only worth carrying out if there is a real issue of origin or process that requires a detailed picture of the dynamic relationships in a suite of samples. In most cases where characterization is all that is needed, finger texturing should be the mainstay of field textural assessment.

2.10 Loss on ignition

Loss on ignition is the main laboratory technique used to measure the organic matter content of soils and sediments. Although many different methods are available, they are all based on the principle that the weight lost on heating is closely correlated with the organic matter content of the sample. Since organic matter accumulates in topsoil, the method is valuable for looking at soil development sequences. In depositional environments, it can be an accurate way of tracking fluctuations between sediment accretion and plant growth in peat beds and estuarine sequences. The resultant data can also be used to examine the sequence for unconformities and hiatuses where rapid changes in organic content may be a result of erosion rather than of a true environmental change. A recommended methodology for loss on ignition can be found in Appendix 1.

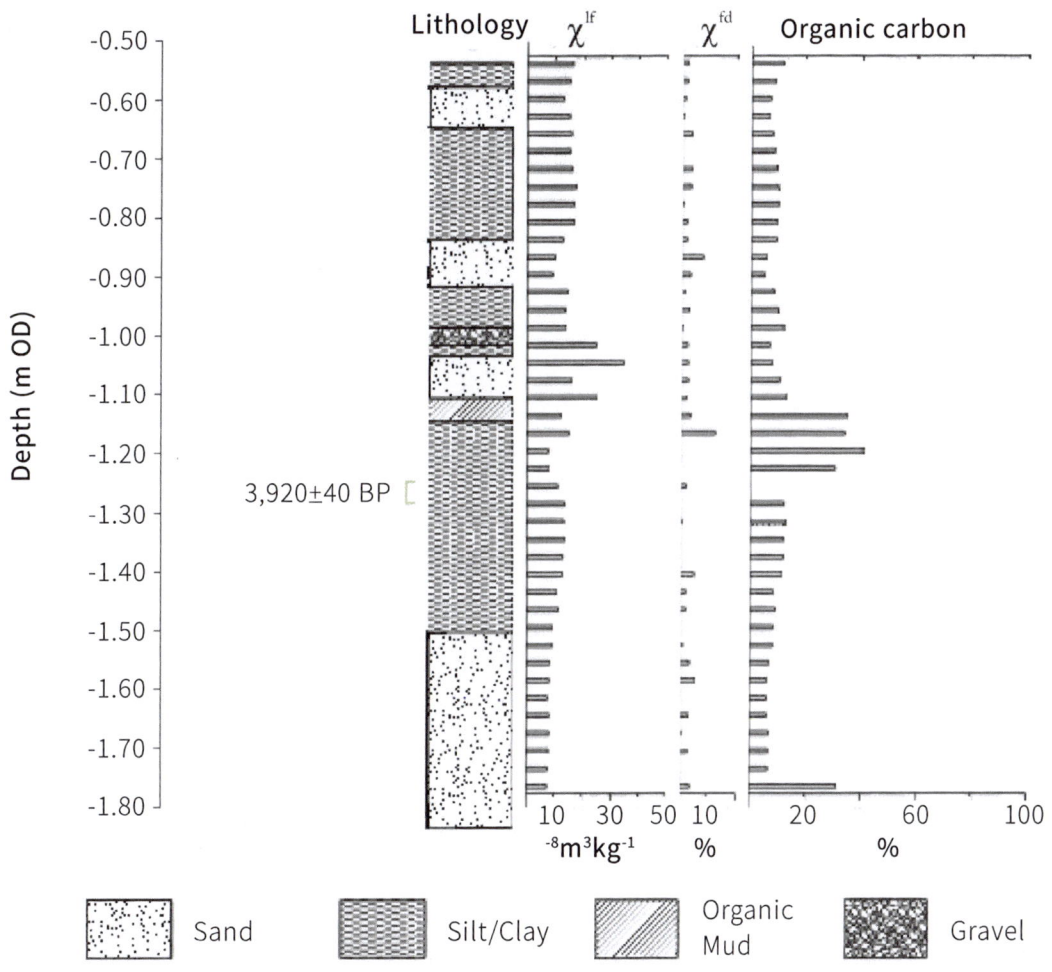

Figure 28
Diagram of texture, low frequency and frequency-dependent magnetic susceptibility, and organic carbon content of sediments from Westminster, London.

2.11 Magnetic susceptibility

Magnetic susceptibility is a measure of the degree to which a sample can be magnetised. This property is affected by numerous natural and anthropogenic factors (Thompson and Oldfield 1986; Gale and Hoare 1991) but is crudely related to soil development and often strongly enhanced by burning or by the addition of heated materials. Therefore, soils or sediments that have undergone these modifications will be distinct from those that have not, and the difference can be easily measured (Fig 28). Patterns of magnetic susceptibility change can thus assist in the correlation of stratigraphic horizons in borehole surveys. Close interval measurement of sedimentary sequences can indicate whether specific events have occurred, or whether the sequence (and presumably site or local area) has remained unchanged over the period in question. Although magnetic susceptibility is more often used as a geophysical prospection tool within archaeology, its value in attempting to locate human activity through time as reflected in deep sequences is becoming more widely known (Walden *et al* 1999, 218–19). A methodology for measuring magnetic susceptibility is presented in Appendix 1.

2.12 pH

The pH of a deposit is a measure of its acidity or alkalinity. This is essentially a broad chemical generalisation, but it can help to understand soil histories and to explain aspects of taphonomy and artefact or ecofact preservation. In general, well-drained siliceous deposits will have acidified over archaeological time scales in the UK climate, while calcareous ones will remain alkaline. In between these two extremes, there is a range of possible outcomes. These include deposits that have remained roughly neutral through the release of fresh calcareous material by weathering, and deposits that remain alkaline for a few thousand years until their calcium carbonate is dissolved, after which they acidify. Each different pH history combines with factors such as waterlogging and redox characteristics to produce a range of preservation conditions that differ between sites and even within the area of a single site (**Campbell** *et al* **2011**, Fig 2). pH is measured using a meter and probe in a suspension of soil in distilled water. Meters need to be regularly calibrated against known standards. Field meters are available, but must be acquired from reliable scientific suppliers. Garden-centre pH meters are highly variable in quality, and should not be used (Table 10).

Table 10: Summary of analytical methods and their archaeological applications			
Analytical method	Scale of investigation	Sample type	Archaeological applications
Particle size analysis	Site specific and regional scale	Bulk samples	- Identification of sediment source areas - Understanding of sedimentary and pedological processes
Loss on ignition	Site specific and occasionally regional scale	Bulk samples	- Identifying soil development sequences - Tracking fluctuations between sediment accretion and peat growth in sea-level studies
Magnetic susceptibility	Site and structure scale	Bulk samples	- Geophysical prospection - Identification of human activity in weakly defined sequences
pH	Mainly site and structure scale; occasionally regional scale	Bulk samples	- Understanding soil history - Taphonomy; artefact and ecofact preservation
Mineralogy	Site and regional scale	Bulk samples	- Identification of sediment origins - Biominerals assist identification of soil or sediment use and history
X-radiography	Site scale	Intact blocks	- Understanding of depositional phases and environments
Micromorphology	Site, structure or feature scale	Intact blocks	- Wide ranging aid to archaeological interpretation of features, structures and sites
Multi-element survey	Regional, site, structure or feature scale	Bulk samples	- Prospection and survey to identify and delimit sites - Determination of activity areas within settlements and sites - Interpretation of individual features and/or deposits
Phosphorus survey	Regional, site, structure or feature scale	Bulk samples	- Prospection and survey to identify and delimit sites - Determination of activity area within settlements and sites - Information on past land-use practices - Interpretation of individual features and/or deposits

2.13 Typical geoarchaeological questions

Throughout this document, emphasis has been placed on a question-led approach to geoarchaeology. This should apply as much to higher level approaches as it does to more detailed site work. At the landscape scale, issues such as the broad archaeological potential of an area, its likely human use and the human impact on topography are all part of the geoarchaeological spectrum. This type of landscape analysis will tend to involve techniques, such as borehole surveys and air-photo interpretation, that inform at a suitable scale. Focussing in at the scale of individual deposits, geoarchaeological questions are commonly detailed points of stratigraphic distinction or site formation. Table 11 presents examples of typical site issues that geoarchaeologists are regularly asked to deal with. The methods suggested for answering them are restricted to those from geoarchaeology, when in reality a range of other environmental methods might contribute to resolving some of the issues (Campbell *et al* 2011). It is important to emphasise that field examination is the primary approach in most cases, with subsidiary tests employed only where they are needed.

Table 11:
Example question
Is this reddening due to burning?
Is the contact between these two layers representative of a natural depositional environment or has the upper layer been dumped?
Is this layer visually different due to soil processes or is it a different context?
This layer seems ashy. Was it originally ash?
Is the microstratigraphy intact or bioturbated?
Was this an animal pen?
Is this a buried soil?
Is this a whole soil profile or was it truncated prior to burial?
Were there stillstand phases in this stratigraphic build-up?
Was this a trampled layer or even a floor?
Could this layer have been formed by the washing out of fines from nearby (eg road-wash)?
Where did this silty layer come from?
Is this the natural?
Is this a water-laid deposit?

Common questions and possible geoarchaeological solutions	
Geoarchaeological techniques	**Reference section**
■ Macro-examination of section and field description ■ Magnetic susceptibility to look for enhancement ■ Possible micromorphology of boundary between reddened and normal soil to determine whether the colouration could result from redox-induced mottling, soil heated elsewhere and dumped, or soil heated *in situ*	■ Effects of burning
■ Close field inspection, possibly followed by micromorphology of the contact. Are there portions of the lower layer in the upper layer or vice versa? If so, is this due to bioturbation?	■ Boundary characteristics
■ Field description primarily, possibly followed up by micromorphology for examining matrix differences. Are they similar materials with, for example, iron movement having changed the visual properties?	■ Field description ■ Micromorphology
■ Micromorphology to show remains of ash (characteristic crystals and phytoliths) partly dissolved and not visible at the field scale	■ Micromorphology
■ X-radiography or micromorphology for burrow structures in sediments or faecal remains from soil fauna. Whole layers of soils are sometimes faecal material	■ X-radiography ■ Micromorphology
■ Examination of deposit subsoil interface ■ Phosphate survey of target area and surroundings ■ Micromorphology for calcium carbonate residues and faecal spherulites	■ Boundary characteristics ■ Soil phosphorus analysis ■ Micromorphology
■ Visual inspection of possible horizonation compared to local soils ■ Magnetic susceptibility and loss on ignition useful in some cases ■ Micromorphology to clarify some aspects of soil processes	■ Field description ■ Magnetic susceptibility ■ Loss on ignition ■ Micromorphology
■ Examination for comparison with expected profile in the area, possibly followed by micromorphology if translocations or accumulations (eg illuvial clay) are expected	■ Field description ■ Micromorphology
■ Field description, followed possibly by x-radiography, magnetic susceptibility ■ Micromorphology for evidence of humic materials, weathering, magnetic enhancement, faecal remains or biominerals	■ Field description ■ X-radiography ■ Magnetic susceptibility ■ Micromorphology
■ Micromorphology for compaction structures ■ Particle size for comparison if floor is suspected to be composed of imported material	■ Micromorphology ■ Particle size analysis
■ Particle size for comparison of the fine materials in each layer, and/or micromorphology of the contact	■ Particle size analysis ■ Micromorphology
■ Visual comparison with likely source materials from the surrounding landscape ■ Particle size and heavy mineral analysis of likely candidates	■ Field description ■ Particle size analysis ■ Mineralogy
■ Visual examination ■ Possibly particle size and mineralogy in difficult cases	■ Field description ■ Particle size analysis ■ Mineralogy
■ Visual examination for sorting and lamination ■ Micromorphology useful in some cases	■ Field description ■ Micromorphology

3 Project Organisation and Planning

3.1 Planning and costs

The range of activities discussed above has to be planned for in quite different ways. The predictable needs of a project are often surveys carried out as an integral part of evaluation or run concurrently with the excavation. Borehole work, for example, is sometimes used for geomorphological investigation (eg location of palaeochannels) and may be central to an evaluation strategy as well. This type of need can be planned for and accurately costed early in a project's life (*see above*, Geoarchaeological approaches to stratigraphy). At the other end of the spectrum, completely unpredictable geoarchaeological requirements arise during excavation. Examples of the type of ad hoc problem that geoarchaeologists regularly deal with are given in Table 11; they represent, essentially, stratigraphic questions that many

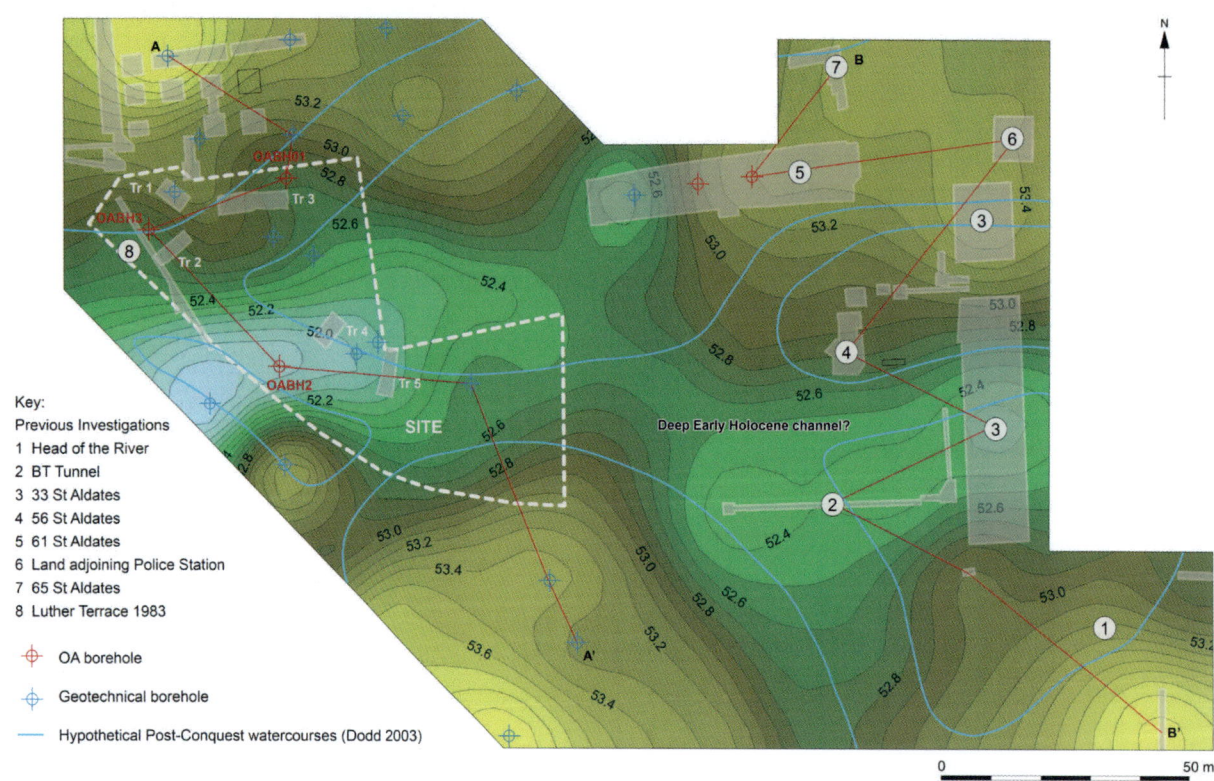

Figure 29
Elevation model of Pleistocene gravel surface showing borehole locations and previous archaeological investigations at Luther Terrace, Oxford.
© Oxford Archaeology

excavators feel unqualified to resolve. Such issues commonly require only on-site advice by the specialist, followed perhaps by a short report to clarify matters on paper. More rarely, sampling will be needed for one of the techniques described in Geoarchaeological approaches to stratigraphy. When this happens, the unpredicted costs will start to become an issue. While still at the excavation stage, these costs may not be too problematic; field sampling for geoarchaeological methods is generally cheap, entailing mostly the use of site equipment, monolith tins for sediment studies and Kubiena tins for micromorphology. Costs are much higher in the laboratory, however, and for this reason, close liaison between the specialist and project director is important to avoid misunderstanding or disappointment. The specialist's ideas of what can be determined in the laboratory need to be rigorously matched with the director's ideas on what is needed for the project aims before money is committed. Because of the potential transience of questions that emerge during excavation, it is especially important that agreements to carry out analysis are revisited after any significant alterations are made to interpretations of the relevant parts of the stratigraphy. This process should happen automatically if the MoRPHE procedure is followed (see www.historicengland.org.uk/images-books/publications/morphe-project-managers-guide).

3.2 Geoarchaeology at different stages of a project

Most archaeological projects involve geoarchaeology as a component part, rather than being entirely geoarchaeology based. It is always useful to have a geoarchaeologist involved at the outset of any project to establish the scope and likely costs of the necessary work, as well as to view the site and select the best approach. Failure to do this simple activity can lead to inappropriate methods and funding miscalculations; often too high as well as too low.

3.3 Desk-top assessment

Geoarchaeologists can contribute to desktop assessments with information about the geological and topographic history of an area and through examination of geotechnical data often supplied by the developer. This can be used to identify areas of archaeological potential and model the sub-surface stratigraphy of the site in order to locate evaluation trenches or borehole positions (Fig 29).

3.4 Evaluation

Evaluations often have a large geoarchaeological component and are the one stage of developer-funded projects that may be conducted entirely using geoarchaeological approaches. This tends to be the case where the relevant sequences are too deeply buried for trenching, or where relatively little archaeology is anticipated. Coring may be used to examine the stratigraphy and collect samples to characterise site formation processes, chronology and the environmental conditions present on site. Selection of drilling method will be assisted by information about likely depth of stratigraphy (the developer should have this information) and the type of sampling required (*see above*, Coring). This should be undertaken by the geoarchaeologist or a commercial company in conjunction with the geoarchaeologist, and the project manager can ensure that support in the form of surveying, photography and health and safety systems are in place. It is possible that a project may not go on to full excavation, for a variety of reasons, such as limited archaeology or a change of development plan. In this case sampling the site during evaluation can provide the only information recovered from the site and could be worthy of further analysis. If the decision is made to excavate, and if better deposits are available, then the evaluation samples can always be discarded. Where no physical traces of human occupation are encountered during the evaluation, it may still be possible to gain useful information about the site through geoarchaeological methods. This obviously needs to be discussed with the local curatorial team, and will be dependent on their view of what is acceptable within the funding. Examination of the stratigraphic sequence can provide good information on the local site formation processes, and this could be of considerable importance at a later date, when interpreting archaeological information from other parts of the area.

3.5 Excavation

Generally, excavation presents wider opportunities for geoarchaeological sampling and it is important that the director remains in contact with the geoarchaeologist to discuss new features as they appear, to arrange site visits or to discuss modifications to the agreed sampling strategy as the excavation progresses. Sampling will often need to be done at short notice (eg if a thin floor being rapidly excavated requires soil micromorphological sampling). Before the excavation starts, it is important for the geoarchaeologist and site director to agree a period of reasonable availability for site visits and sampling.

3.6 Assessment

Geoarchaeological techniques are frequently ill-suited to the typical procedures of assessment of archaeological potential. In the main, geoarchaeological samples cannot be scanned as is the case with an assemblage of, for example, bones. A pragmatic approach will be needed in order to best fulfil the needs of the assessment (Canti 1996), and the level of work undertaken is generally determined by the nature of the scheme and funding. Field description is essential at the assessment stage, but the precise degree of analytical work will vary from project to project. It may be a very basic appraisal of the overall sample assemblage, or actual analysis of a proportion of the samples. Whatever the approach, it should be sufficient to establish potential to address research questions, and must obviously be decided in close consultation with the rest of the excavation team in order to get the best information. The assessment report should contain the proposal for analysis (if appropriate), including all individual tasks and costing. It is important to take into account things such as bench fees if the work is being done in borrowed laboratory space, as well as costs for consumables such as chemicals. In addition to the task list, it is worth considering at this stage whether separate publication from the main report is necessary. The assessment report should therefore include:

- specialist aims and objectives relevant to the project research design

- assessment methods with a description of sampling and processing

- standard descriptions of soils and sediments, where needed

- statement of potential to contribute to the project aims

- statement of potential to contribute to research issues of wider significance

- recommendations for future work, including full analysis if applicable

- time required and costing of future work

3.7 Analysis

Analysis tends to be more straightforward than assessment and should have been planned and costed while preparing the updated project design. The geoarchaeologist needs to work closely with the other specialists on the project and should not undertake analysis without detailed site information (including a chronology) from the site director. A full report should be prepared, including methods, sample details, results and interpretations, as well as appropriate supporting data.

3.8 Dissemination and archiving

Stable materials should be placed in a publicly accessible archive. Some samples, such as micromorphology thin sections, cured blocks and dry bulk samples are easily stored with the rest of the physical archive from the site; many other samples, however, are moist and require cold storage. As yet, there is no feasible method to ensure long-term storage of soil and sediment samples, so issues of subsampling the assemblage for cold storage or discarding the samples will need to be considered. All record sheets and notes should go to the archiving body, in accordance with their standards, and a report produced. Ideally, this will end up being integrated with the full site publication. It may not always be feasible to integrate the whole geoarchaeological report, and alternative publications may be needed, for example in archaeological journals, earth science journals or conference proceedings.

4 Where to Get Advice

Numerous individuals and organisations can help with one or other of the activities or requirements described above. Some specialise in laboratory analyses, others in chemical survey, in borehole work or other methods. Furthermore, there is considerable growth in the numbers of people involved as recently qualified geoarchaeologists emerge from universities. It is, therefore, impossible to produce a list of specialists without missing some people out, introducing bias or apparent recommendation. Once an area of requirement has been isolated from the range discussed in this document, it is suggested that the first person to contact should be the Historic England Regional Science Advisor who will be able to provide an updated list of names and contact numbers for the relevant specialists. Contact details can be found at http://HistoricEngland.org.uk/advice/technical-advice/archaeological-science/science-advisors/

4.1 The Regional Science Advisors are currently (2015)

East of England
Mark Ruddy
Cambridge Office
Tel: 01223 582707
Email: Mark.Ruddy@HistoricEngland.org.uk

East Midlands Region
Jim Williams
Northampton Office
Tel: 01454 419228
Mob: 07801 213300
Email: Jim.Williams@HistoricEngland.org.uk

London
Sylvia Warman
London Office
Tel: 0207 973 3733
Mob: 07881 805347
Email: Sylvia.Warman@HistoricEngland.org.uk

North East Region
Jacqui Huntley
Newcastle Office
Tel: 0191 269 1250
Mob: 07713 400387
Email: Jacqui.Huntley@HistoricEngland.org.uk

North West Region
Sue Stallibrass
Manchester Office
Tel: 0151 794 5046,
Mob: 07867 551887
Email: Sue.Stallibrass@HistoricEngland.org.uk

South East Region
Jane Corcoran
Guildford Office
Tel: 01483 252072
Mob: 07879 809294
Email: Jane.Corcoran@HistoricEngland.org.uk

South West Region
Vanessa Straker
Bristol Office
Tel: 0117 975 0689
Mob: 07789 745054
Email: Vanessa.Straker@HistoricEngland.org.uk

West Midlands Region
Lisa Moffett
Birmingham Office
Tel: 0121 625 6875
Mob: 07769 960022
Email: Lisa.Moffett@HistoricEngland.org.uk

Yorkshire Region
Andy Hammon
York Office
Tel: 01904 601983
Mob: 07747 486255
Email: Andy.Hammon@HistoricEngland.org.uk

Alternatively, there is currently one member of Historic England laboratory staff who can offer impartial opinions, advice on geoarchaeological issues and how to locate suitable specialists:

Matthew Canti
Fort Cumberland
Fort Cumberland Road
Eastney
Portsmouth
PO4 9LD
Tel: 02392 856775
Email: Matt.Canti@HistoricEngland.org.uk

https://HistoricEngland.org.uk/research/approaches/research-methods/Archaeology/geoarchaeology/

Sassa http://www.sassa.org.uk/index.php/Soil_Analysis_Support_System_for_Archaeology

As well as the advisory network described above, there is a free internet-based system based in StirlingUniversity. Sassa is designed to familiarise archaeologists with the concepts of geoarchaeology, as well as providing an XML tool to help standardise descriptions and assist with interpretations.

Appendix 1: Methods

A1 Finger texturing (Fig 30)

Take a small quantity of soil, about the size of a marble, and moisten if necessary. Work between the fingers until it is reasonably uniform, then run through these questions:

1. Can the soil be rolled into a ball?
   yes .... go to 2
   no .... Sand

2. Can the soil be rolled into a thick (10–15mm) sausage between the palms?
   yes .... go to 3
   no .... Loamy Sand

3. Can the soil be rolled into a thin (c 5mm) sausage between the palms?
   yes .... go to 4
   no .... Sandy Loam

4. Can the thin sausage be bent into a U shape without cracking?
   yes .... go to 5
   no, and feels gritty .... Sandy Silt Loam
   no and feels doughy .... Silt Loam

5. Can the thin sausage be bent into a ring without cracking?
   yes .... go to 7
   no .... go to 6

6. Does the soil feel very gritty? .. Sandy Clay Loam
   slightly gritty? .... Clay Loam
   like dough? .... Silty Clay Loam

7. Does a surface rubbed with finger and thumb become:
   very smooth and very polished? .... Clay
   smooth and slightly polished? .... Silty Clay
   smooth with sand grains visible? ...... Sandy Clay

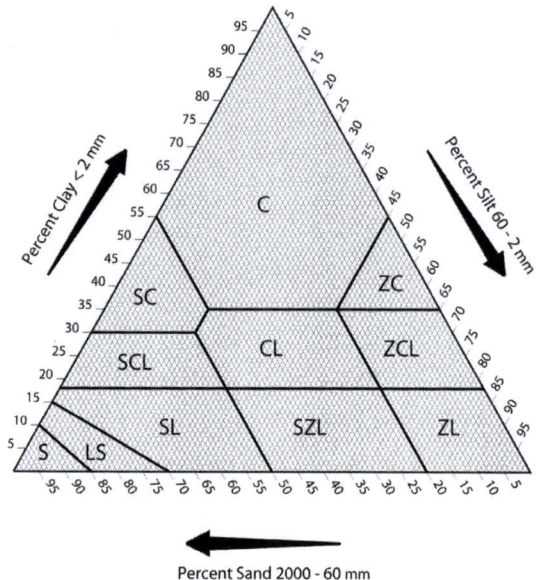

Figure 30
The soil textural triangle.

A2 Troels-Smith description

The Troels-Smith system (Troels-Smith 1955) relies on encoding stratigraphy with descriptors for both physical characteristics and sedimentary components. These are broken down using a form of Latin nomenclature, making the system truly international. It is semi-objective and relies solely on description with no interpretation of sedimentary process, making it suitable both for field and laboratory use and also avoiding problems when trying to re-interpret a sequence. In addition to the Latin terms, there is a series of symbols by which the sediment types may be represented. The description of physical characteristics includes darkness, stratification, elasticity, dryness, and boundary. These are scored from 0 to 4 – for example, a clean chalk unit would obtain a darkness score of 0. Sedimentary components are described within categories of organic and mineral types. The mineral types are generally classed by particle size, with additional categories for soil and sediment with calcareous and iron oxide inclusions. The organic types are broken down further into detrital and in situ deposits, then classified by type of plant and the size of fragments. Each sedimentary unit achieves a score of 4 in the classification of components. For instance a pure clay would score AS 4 (argilla steatodes – colloids or grains <0.002mm), while a degraded detrital wood peat might score SH 2 (substantia humosa – unidentifiable organic matter) DL 2 (detritus lignosus – superterranean fragments of ligneous plants >2mm). The system has some drawbacks, for example different particle size grades to the widely-used system, and the fact that the description of contact between sedimentary units is simply a measure of the thickness of the transition zone; however, additional comments may be added to the description of the unit (Table 12).

A3 Magnetic susceptibility

In most cases, the sample should be initially air dried at temperatures of <40° C in order to avoid affecting its magnetic properties. It is then ground in a mortar and pestle, sieved through a 2mm mesh and placed according to coil size into numbered 100ml or 10ml plastic, lidded

Table 12: Deposit elements described by the modified Troels-Smith method (Aaby and Berglund 1986)			
	Sh	Substantia humosa	Humus substance, homogeneous microscopic structure
I Turf	Tb $^{0-4}$	T. bryophytica	Mosses +/- humus substance
	Tl $^{0-4}$	T. lignosa	Stumps, roots, intertwined rootlets of ligneous plants +/- trunks, stems, branches, etc connected with these +/- humus substance
	Th $^{0-4}$	T. herbacea	Roots, intertwined rootlets, rhizomes of herbaceous plants +/- stems, leaves, etc connected with these +/- humus substance
II Detritus	Dl	D. lignosus	Fragments of ligneous plants > 2mm
	Dh	D. herbosus	Fragments of herbaceous plants > 2mm
	Dg	D. granosus	Fragments of ligneous and herbaceous plants and sometimes of animal fossils (except molluscs) < 2mm > c 0.1mm
III Limus	Ld $^{0-4}$	L. detrituosus	Plants and animals (except diatoms, needles of spongi, siliceous skeletons, etc. Of organic origin), or fragments of these; particles < c 0.1mm. +/- Humus substance
	Lso	L. siliceus organogenes	Diatoms, needles of spongi, siliceous skeletons, etc. Of organic origin or part of these; particles < c 0.1mm
	Lc	L. calcareus	Marl, not hardened like calcareous tufa; lime and the like; particles < c 0.1mm
	Lf	L. ferrugineus	Rust, not hardened; particles < c 0.1mm
IV Argilla	As	A steatodes	Particles of clay < 0.002mm
	Ag	A. granosa	Particles of silt 0.06-0.002mm
V Grana	Gmin	G. minora	Particles of sand 2-0.06mm
	Gmaj	G. majora	Particles of gravel 60-2mm

pots (weighed to two decimal places). The pot, lid and sample are then re-weighed together. Care should be taken with samples from waterlogged deposits that may contain a significant quantity of unstable iron minerals, such as greigite, and thus could be affected by oxidation during air drying. In this case, measurements should be made immediately on the wet samples followed by air drying to determine the dry mass of the sample. The analytical procedure follows that of Gale and Hoare (1991, 204–20) for low frequency (χlf) measurement, using a purpose-built Bartington magnetic susceptibility sensor and meter. Prior to each run of samples, the meter is zeroed and an air blank is measured. Air blanks do not always register zero, owing to factors such as air movement, temperature swings and machine drift. The sample is placed in the meter, measured on low frequency for about 10 seconds, then removed and a further air blank taken. The drift factors may continue to operate while the actual magnetic susceptibility sample is being measured; hence the need for the two blanks. The two measured values are then combined, a mean calculated and the resulting value is removed from the actual magnetic susceptibility reading. In addition, laboratory samples may be remeasured at a higher frequency of AC magnetising field to determine the frequency dependence of magnetic susceptibility. Frequency dependence increases with the concentration of ultrafine magnetic particles – often produced through burning – and may be useful for detecting burnt material.

Loss on ignition

Loss on ignition procedures are detailed by Gale and Hoare (1991, 262–4).The samples should be dried at 105° C and weighed, then placed in weighed (to three decimal places), numbered porcelain crucibles. The crucible and sample should be re-weighed together and then fired in a muffle furnace at 430° C for 24 hours. After cooling in a desiccator, the crucibles and remaining sediment should be reweighed and the weight loss expressed as a percentage of the original sediment weight to provide the organic matter content. Loss on ignition can be carried out at a higher temperature for a shorter time (eg 550° C for 4 hours) where samples do not contain calcium carbonate, but this is not an easy variable to assess, so the longer burn is the safer procedure.

Figure 31
Two examples of the spot-test for soil phosphorus analysis: the length and colour intensity of blue rays radiating out from the soil sample are used to provide a qualitative assessment of the concentration of phosphorus present.

Spot-test for phosphorus

This low-cost test can be carried out rapidly on site, so the results can be fed back directly into survey or excavation strategies as they happen. The test requires that two solutions be prepared, both of which can safely be used in the field. It should be noted that Solution A is stable for about one month, while a fresh batch of Solution B must be prepared daily:

Solution A: dissolve 5g ammonium molybdate in 100ml distilled cold water then acidify by adding 30ml of 5N hydrochloric acid

Solution B: dissolve 1g ascorbic acid in 200ml cold distilled water

To carry out the test, a small amount of soil (c 5g) is placed onto ash-free filter paper and two drops of Solution A applied. After 30 seconds, two drops of Solution B are added and if phosphorus is present in the sample, a blue colour will begin to develop on the filter paper around the soil sample. The intensity of the colouration is taken as a reflection of the amount of phosphorus present in the sample (Fig 31 and Table 13). However, the colour development is also time dependent and the reaction time should therefore be standardised (eg always take the reading exactly two minutes after the application of Solution B). The reaction can be stopped at this stage by immersing the filter paper in a solution of sodium citrate (ratio of 2:1 water to sodium citrate; see Eidt 1977). This fixes the reaction, after which the filter papers can be stored and labelled, thus producing an archive of the results. It should be stressed that the spot-test is only appropriate for fairly coarse applications, particularly prospection and low resolution survey work, where it will be most successful if used in conjunction with other techniques such as aerial reconnaissance and borehole survey. Where phosphorus analysis is to be used for high-resolution intra-site analysis then quantitative methods should be applied.

Table 13: Relative grading for degree of colour development and interpretative meaning (after Schwartz 1967)		
Value	Descriptor	Observations
0	Negative	No blue tint visible
1	Trace	Blue tint develops up to 2mm from sample with discrete blue rays
2	Weak	Blue tint forms circle around sample with individual rays bleeding together
3	Positive	Distinct blue band with diameter c 10–15mm develops around sample
4	Strong	Large blue spot of c 20mm diameter or greater

Appendix 2: Glossary of Terms

aeolian an adjective meaning 'of wind', but also sometimes used as 'windblown'

alluvium any water-borne sediment is technically alluvium, but the common usage is for fine-grained floodplain deposits

bedding sedimentary structures visible in sections and characteristic of particular depositional environments

bioturbation the disruption and movement of deposits by biological processes

boulder clay a deposit derived directly or indirectly from the action of ice-masses during glacial episodes; may contain all the particle sizes from boulders down to clay particles. Boulder clay mantles much of northern and eastern England

brickearth a functional name (the material was used in the past to make bricks) for silt deposits found in some river valleys. The origin is probably redeposited loess

brown earth the commonest soil type with a dark mull humus topsoil over a deep brown subsoil and developed on well-drained circum-neutral parent materials

calcium carbonate common earth surface compound ($CaCO_3$) precipitated in marine and pedological situations. It is also widely utilised by animals to form shell, and thus ends up as a major component of chalk and other limestones

calcium phosphate biologically precipitated compound ($CaPO_4$), most commonly occurring in bone, but also crystallising occasionally in nutrient-rich situations (eg cess pits)

chalk soft form of limestone

clay mineral particles smaller than 0.002mm

colluvium soil or sediment material that accumulates at the bottom of a slope. Colluvium can be several metres deep, and is usually poorly sorted with either weak, or no stratification

cryoturbation disruption and movement of deposits by periglacial processes, especially by freeze and thaw

dark earth term for dark coloured, poorly-stratified soil deposits sometimes found overlying Roman stratigraphy

diatom aquatic algae leaving behind identifiable silica skeletons

dry valley a valley with no stream in it, common in areas with chalk bedrock

earthworm granules distinctive aggregates of calcium carbonate produced by earthworms, typically less than 2.5mm

eluviation washing out of fine material from a horizon in a soil profile (generally downwards)

faecal spherulites distinctive microscopic calcium carbonate features formed in the gut of some animals and preserved in neutral to alkaline stratigraphy

feldspar a common group of minerals formed of potassium, calcium or sodium aluminium silicates

foraminifera marine organisms (predominantly) depositing diagnostic tests (shells) that are typically microscopic

gley a soil whose major characteristic is that it is waterlogged for all or part of the time

granulometry another term for particle size analysis

greigite a form of iron sulphide

gypsum calcium sulphate ($CaSO_4.2H_2O$) often formed in marshy and peaty situations where sulphides have oxidized in the presence of calcium carbonate

heavy minerals minerals that sink in the bromine-based heavy liquids (in which common quartz floats)

illuviation washing in of fine material from higher up in a soil profile

iron oxides common earth surface compounds arising from weathering. Three widespread forms are lepidocrocite, goethite and haematite, which colour soils yellow, brown and red, respectively

jarosite potassium iron sulphate mineral composed of $KFe_3(SO_4)2.(OH)_6$, and deposited where iron sulphides have oxidised in the absence of calcium carbonate; typically found in sediments associated with salt water

Kubiena tin a small (c 10cm x 7cm) metal box used for micromorphology sampling

levee a raised bank close to a river channel

limestone sedimentary rocks composed mostly of calcium carbonate

loam a class of texture containing moderate amounts of sand, silt and clay

loess wind-blown silt

loss on ignition the weight loss from low-temperature burning of soil, correlating well with the organic matter content

lynchet a bank caused by movement of soil down-slope and its accumulation against a barrier such as a wall or hedge

magnetic susceptibility the degree to which a sample will become magnetized when placed in a magnetic field

marl term for silty sediments, usually applied to calcareous lake deposits

micromorphology the microscopic analysis of thin sections of resin impregnated stratigraphy

mor humus a form of topsoil occurring in acidic situations where organic matter forms a dark surface mat, rather than being intimately mixed with the mineral material

mull humus the common form of topsoil showing mineral and organic matter intimately mixed by biological activity

organic matter all dead plant and animal matter in soils and sediments

oxidation the process of conversion to oxides, which happens in moist aerated environments. Organic materials become carbon dioxide and water; iron becomes rust

pal(a)eosol a soil that has developed in a past landscape and that may be buried or exposed

particle size the distribution of stones, sand, silt and clay in a deposit

periglacial the descriptive term for the cold climatic conditions, the characteristic landforms and the sediments found in areas adjacent to ice sheets

pH a measure of the acidity or alkalinity of a soil or sediment

phosphates compounds whose anion is composed of phosphorus and oxygen (usually PO_4)

phytolith microscopic mineral body (usually silica) found in many plants and often preserved in stratigraphy

podzol a leached soil, usually on sandy acid parent materials. It has a mor humus topsoil overlying characteristically bleached sand

pyrite the commonest iron sulphide ($FeS2$) mineral

quartz the main form of silica in soils and sediments

redox shorthand term for the general oxidation-reduction state of a deposit

reduction the process of losing oxygen to form reduced compounds. Reduction happens in wet, low oxygen environments. Organic compounds blacken and become stable; sulphur-rich compounds form iron sulphide (commonly pyrite) or hydrogen sulphide (a gas smelling of rotten eggs); and iron compounds turn green and become soluble

rendzina a thin dark soil usually developed on soft limestone

saltation process whereby wind-blown particles move in discrete jumps rather than staying constantly airborne

sand mineral particles of 2mm to 0.063mm

sediment a collection of rock, mineral and/or organic particles that has been moved from their original source and redeposited elsewhere by natural or human agencies

shale laminated sedimentary rock formed of compressed silt and clay

silica silicon dioxide (SiO_2). Silica forms the main constituent of sand (as quartz) and the commonest type of phytolith

silt mineral particles of 0.063mm to 0.002mm

slate fine-grained laminar rock produced by pressure and heat during geological processes

soil loose material at the earth's surface undergoing weathering and horizon formation owing to hydration, redox processes and the accumulation of organic matter from organisms that live within it

sorting measure of the degree to which the particles in a sediment are concentrated in one size grouping

taphonomy study of post-depositional processes

tephra volcanic ash

test type of shell (typically of foraminifera)

testate amoebae organisms that live in peat and leave behind identifiable microscopic protein and silica tests

texture the property resulting from the relative proportions of sand, silt and clay in a soil or sediment – same as particle size

till another word for boulder clay

unconformity boundary between two layers where the earlier layer can be seen to have been eroded before deposition of the later layer

vivianite an iron phosphate mineral $Fe_3(PO_4)2.8H_2O$ that crystallises in reduced, biologically rich environments. On exposure to air, it can turn to a strikingly blue powder

Bibliography

Aaby, B and Berglund, B E 1986 'Characterization of peat and lake deposits', in Berglund, B E (ed) *Handbook of Holocene Palaeoecology and Palaeohydrology*. London: John Wiley and Sons, 231-42

Allen, M J 1992 'Products of erosion and the prehistoric land-use of the Wessex chalk', in Bell, M and Boardman, J (eds) *Past and Present Soil Erosion*. Oxford: Oxbow Monograph **22**, 37-52

Allen, T and Welsh, K 1996 'Eton Rowing Lake'. *Current Archaeology* **148**, 124-7

Aston, M A, Martin, M H and Jackson, A W 1998 'The potential for heavy metal soil analysis on low status archaeological sites at Shapwick, Somerset'. *Antiquity* **72**, 838-47

Bates, M R and Bates, C R 2000. 'Multidisciplinary approaches to the geoarchaeological evaluation of deeply stratified sedimentary sequences: examples from Pleistocene and Holocene deposits in southern England, United Kingdom'. *Journal of Archaeological Science* **27**, 845-58

Bates, M R and Stafford, E 2013 *Thames Holocene: A geoarchaeological approach to the investigation of the river floodplain for High Speed 1, 1994-2004*. Salisbury: Wessex Archaeology

Bell, M 1977 *Excavation at Bishopstone*. Lewes: Sussex Archaeological Collections **115**

BMAPA and English Heritage 2003 'Marine Aggregate Dredging and the Historic Environment'. London: British Marine Aggregate Producers Association and English Heritage http://www.wessexarch.co.uk/files/projects/BMAPA-Protocol/BMAPA-EH-Guidance-Note-April-2003.pdf

Bridges, E M 1997 *World Soils*. Cambridge: Cambridge University Press

Bridgland, D R 1994 *Quaternary of the Thames. Geological Conservation Review*, Joint Nature Conservation Committee. London: Chapman and Hall

— 2001 'The Pleistocene evolution and Palaeolithic occupation of the Solent river', in Hosfield, R T and Wenban-Smith, F (eds) *Palaeolithic archaeology of the Solent river*, 15-25. Lithic Studies Society Occasional Papers **7**

Brown, A G 1992 'Slope erosion and colluviation at the floodplain edge', *in* Bell, M and Boardman, J (eds) *Past and Present Soil Erosion*. Oxford: Oxbow Monograph **22**, 77-87

— 1997 *Alluvial Geoarchaeology: Floodplain Archaeology and Environmental Change*. Cambridge: Cambridge University Press

Campbell, G, Moffett, L and Straker, V 2011 'Environmental Archaeology. A Guide to the Theory and Practice of Methods, from Sampling and Recovery to Post-excavation (second edition)'. Portsmouth: English Heritage https://content.historicengland.org.uk/images-books/publications/environmental-archaeology-2nd/environmental-archaeology-2nd.pdf/

Canti, M G 1992 '*Research into natural and anthropogenic deposits from the excavations at Flixborough, Humberside*'. Ancient Monuments Laboratory Report **53/92**. London: English Heritage http://research.historicengland.org.uk/redirect.aspx?id=4261

— 1996 '*Guidelines for carrying out assessments in geoarchaeology*'. Ancient Monuments Laboratory Report **34/96**. London: English Heritage http://research.historicengland.org.uk/redirect.aspx?id=4575

— 2003 'Earthworm activity and archaeological stratigraphy: a review of products and processes'. *Journal of Archaeological Science* **30**, 135-48

Canti, M G and Linford, N 2000 'The effects of fire on archaeological soils and sediments: temperature and colour relationships'. *Proceedings of the Prehistoric Society* **66**, 385-95

Canti, M G and Meddens, F M 1998 'Mechanical coring as an aid to archaeological projects'. *Journal of Field Archaeology* **25**, 97-105 http://www.jstor.org/stable/530460?seq=1#page_scan_tab_contents

Carruthers, W J 2000 'Mineralised plant remains', *in* Lawson, AJ (ed) *Potterne 1982-5: Animal Husbandry in Later Prehistoric Wiltshire*. Wessex Archaeology Report **17**, 72-83

Carter, S 2001 'A reassessment of the origins of the St Andrews "garden soil"'. *Tayside and Fife Archaeological Journal* **7**, 87-92

Catt, J A 1999 'Particle size distribution and mineralogy of the deposits', *in* Roberts, M and Parfitt, S A Boxgrove: A Middle P*leistocene Hominid Site at Eartham Quarry, Boxgrove, West Sussex*. London: English Heritage Archaeological Report **17**, 111-18

Coles, J and Coles, B 1986 *Sweet track to Glastonbury*. London: Thames and Hudson

Conway, J S 1983 'An investigation of soil phosphorus distribution within occupation deposits from a Romano- British hut group'. *Journal of Archaeological Science* **10**, 117-28

Corcoran, J, Halsey, C, Spurr, G, Burton, E and Jamieson, D 2011 *Mapping past landscapes in the lower Lea valley : A geoarchaeological study of the Quaternary sequence*. MOLA Monograph **55**. London: Museum of London Archaeology

Courty, M A, Goldberg, P and Macphail, R I, 1989 *Soils and Micromorphology in Archaeology*. Cambridge: Cambridge University Press

Craddock, P T, Gurney, D, Pryor, F and Hughes, M J 1985 'The application of phosphate analysis to the location and interpretation of archaeological sites'. *Archaeological Journal* **142**, 361-76

Davidson, D A and Simpson, IA 2001 'Archaeology and soil micromorphology', *in* Brothwell, D R and Pollard, A M (eds) *Handbook of Archaeological Sciences*. Chichester: Wiley, 167-77

Eidt, R 1977 'Detection and examination of anthrosols by phosphate analysis'. *Science* **197**, 1327-33

English Heritage 2006 *Science for Historic Industries*. Swindon: English Heritage. https://historicengland.org.uk/images-books/publications/science-for-historic-industries/

Entwistle, J and Abrahams, PW 1998 'Multi-elemental analysis of soils and sediments from Scottish archaeological sites. The potential of inductively-coupled plasma-mass spectrometry for rapid site investigation'. *Journal of Archaeological Science* **24**, 407-16

Fitzpatrick, E A 1980 *Soils: Their Formation, Classification and Distribution*. Harlow: Longman

French, C A I 2003 *Geoarchaeology in Action: Studies in Soil Micromorphology and Landscape Evolution*. London: Routledge

Gale, S J and Hoare, P G 1991 *Quaternary Sediments: Petrographic Methods for the Study of Unlithified Rocks*. London: Belhaven Press

Goudie, A S and Brunsden, D 1994 *The Environment of the British Isles: An Atlas*. Oxford: Clarendon Press

Greatorex, C 2003 'Living on the margins? The Late Bronze Age landscape of the Willingdon Levels', *in* Rudling, D (ed) *The Archaeology of Sussex to AD2000*. King's Lynn: Heritage Marketing, 89-100

Gribble, J and Leather, S 2011 'Offshore Geotechnical Investigations and Historic Environment Analysis: Guidance for the Renewable Energy Sector'. Commissioned by COWRIE Ltd. http://www.thecrownestate.co.uk/media/5876/km-ex-pc-historic-012007-historic-environment-guidance-for-the-offshore-renewable-energy-sector.pdf

Gurney, D A 1985 *Phosphate Analysis of Soils: A Guide for the Field Archaeologist*. Institute of Field Archaeologists Technical Paper **3**

Hawkes, S C 1968 'The physical geography of Richborough', *in* Cunliffe, B W (ed) *Fifth Report on the Excavations of the Roman Fort at Richborough, Kent. Report of the Research Committee of the Society of Antiquaries of London* **23**, 224-31

Heathcote, J 2000 'Soil micromorphology', *in* Rippon, S 'The Romano-British Exploitation of Coastal Wetlands: Survey and Excavation on the North Somerset Levels, 1993-7'. *Britannia* **31**, 107-12

Historic England 2015 *Archaeometallurgy: guidelines for best practice*. Swindon: Historic England. https://historicengland.org.uk/images-books/publications/archaeometallurgy-guidelines-best-practice/

Hodgkinson, D, Huckerby, E, Middleton, R, and Wells, C E 2000 *The Lowland Wetlands of Cumbria*. North West Wetlands Survey **6**. University of Lancaster, Lancaster Imprints **8**

Hodgson, J 1976 *Soil Survey Field Handbook*. Soil Survey Technical Monograph **5**. Harpenden: Rothamsted Experimental Station

Howard, A J and Macklin, M G 1999 'A generic geomorphological approach to archaeological interpretation and prospection in British river valleys: a guide for archaeologists investigating Holocene landscapes'. *Antiquity* **73**, 527-41

Hudson-Edwards, K A, Macklin, M G, Finlayson, R and Passmore, D G 1999 'Medieval lead pollution in the River Ouse at York, England'. *Journal of Archaeological Science* **26**, 809-19

Knight, D, and Howard, A J 1995 *Archaeology and Alluvium in the Trent Valley: An Archaeological Assessment of the Floodplain and Gravel Terraces*. Nottingham: Trent and Peak Archaeological Trust

Limbrey, S 1975 *Soil Science and Archaeology*. London: Academic Press

Lippi, R D 1988 'Palaeotopography and P analysis of a buried jungle site in Ecuador'. *Journal of Field Archaeology* **15**, 85-7. http://www.jstor.org/stable/530131

Long, A J 1995 'Sea-level and crustal movements in the Thames estuary, Essex and east Kent', *in* Bridgland, D R, Allen, P and Haggart, B A (eds) *The Quaternary of the Lower Reaches of the Thames*. Durham: Quaternary Research Association, 99-105

Loveluck, C P (ed) 2007 *Rural Settlement, Lifestyles and Social change in the later first millennium AD. Anglo-Saxon Flixborough in its wider context*. Excavations at Flixborough, Volume **4**. Oxford: Oxbow

Payton, R W and Usai, M R 1995 *Assessment of Soils and Sediments from and Exploratory Excavations at Low Hauxley, Northumberland*. York: Reports from the Environmental Archaeology Unit

Plets, R, Dix, J and Bates, R 2013 *Marine Geophysics Data Acquisition, Processing and Interpretation: Guidance notes*. Swindon: English Heritage. https://historicengland.org.uk/images-books/publications/marine-geophysics-data-acquisition-processing-interpretation/

Preece, R C, Bridgland, D R and Sharp, M J 1998 'Stratigraphical investigations', *in* Preece, R C and Bridgland, D R (eds) *Late Quaternary Environmental Change in North-West Europe: Excavations at Holywell Coombe, South-east England*. London: Chapman and Hall, 33-68

Ransley, J, Sturt, F, Dix, J, Adams, J and Blue, L 2013 'People and the Sea: A Maritime Archaeological Research Agenda for England'. Council for British Archaeology, Report **171**. York: CBA

Rapp, G J, and Hill, C H 1998 *Geoarchaeology: the Earth-Science Approach to Archaeological Interpretation*. New Haven: Yale University Press

Rippon, S 1996 *The Gwent Levels: Evolution of a Wetland Landscape*. York: CBA Res Rep **105**

Schwarz, G T 1967 'A simplified chemical test for archaeological fieldwork'. *Archaeometry* **10**, 57-63

Sidell, J, Wilkinson, K, Scaife, R, and Cameron, N 2000 *The Holocene Evolution of the London Thames*. London: Museum of London Monograph **5**

Sieveking, G de G, Longworth, I H, Hughes, M J, Clark, A J and Millett, A 1973 'A new survey of Grime's Graves – first report'. *Proceedings of the Prehistoric Society* **39**, 182-218

Simpson, I A, Milek, K B and Gudmundsson, G 1999 'A reinterpretation of the Great Pit at Hofstadir, Iceland, using sediment thin section micromorphology'. *Geoarchaeology* **14**, 511-30

Spencer, C, Plater, A and Long, A 1998 'Holocene barrier estuary evolution: the sedimentary record of the lower Wall and marsh region', *in* Eddison, J, Gardiner, M and Long, A (eds) *Romney Marsh: Environmental Change and Human Occupation in a Coastal Lowland*. Oxford: OUCA Monograph **46**, 13-29

Swift, D 2007 *Roman Waterfront Development at 12 Arthur Street, City of London*. MOLA Archaeology Studies **19**. London: Museum of London Archaeology

Taylor, M P, and Macklin, M G 1997 'Holocene alluvial sedimentation and valley floor development: the River Swale, Catterick, North Yorkshire, UK'. *Proceedings of the Yorkshire Geological Society* **51**, 317-27

Thompson, R and Oldfield, F 1986 *Environmental Magnetism*. London: Allen and Unwin

Troels-Smith, J 1955. 'Characterisation of unconsolidated sediments'. *Danmarks Geologiske Undersøgelse* **4**, 38-73

Van de Noort, R, and Ellis, S 1998 *Wetland Heritage of the Ancholme and Lower Trent Valleys: An Archaeological Survey*. Hull: Humber Wetlands Project

Walden, J, Oldfield, F, and Smith, J 1999 'Environmental magnetism: a practical guide'. London: Quaternary Research Association Technical Guide **6**

Waller, M 1994 *The Fenland Project, Number 9: Flandrian Environmental Change in Fenland*. East Anglian Archaeology Report **70**. Cambridge: Essex County Council

Wilkinson, K N, Scaife, R G and Sidell, E J 2000 'Environmental and sealevel changes *in* London from 10,500 BP to the present: a case study from Silvertown'. *Proceedings of the Geologists' Association* **111**, 41-54

Acknowledgements

Text compiled by Historic England staff from Fort Cumberland and Regional Science Advisors: M Canti, J Heathcote, G Ayala, J Corcoran and J Sidell.

The authors would like to thank the following people for providing comment on the text: Nick Branch, Tony Brown, Gill Campbell, Peter Clark, Charles French, Richard Havis, Andy Howard, Marcus Jecock, Helen Keeley, Sandy Kidd, David Knight, Tom Lane, Wendy Matthews, Karen Milek, Lisa Moffett, Peter Murphy, Jacqui Nowakowski, David Robinson, Ian Simpson, Vanessa Straker, Keith Wilkinson and Jim Williams.

Contact Historic England

East Midlands
2nd Floor, Windsor House
Cliftonville
Northampton NN1 5BE
Tel: 01604 735460
Email: eastmidlands@HistoricEngland.org.uk

East of England
Brooklands
24 Brooklands Avenue
Cambridge CB2 8BU
Tel: 01223 582749
Email: eastofengland@HistoricEngland.org.uk

Fort Cumberland
Fort Cumberland Road
Eastney
Portsmouth PO4 9LD
Tel: 023 9285 6704
Email: fort.cumberland@HistoricEngland.org.uk

London
1 Waterhouse Square
138-142 Holborn
London EC1N 2ST
Tel: 020 7973 3700
Email: london@HistoricEngland.org.uk

North East
Bessie Surtees House
41-44 Sandhill
Newcastle Upon Tyne
NE1 3JF
Tel: 0191 269 1255
Email: northeast@HistoricEngland.org.uk

North West
3rd Floor, Canada House
3 Chepstow Street
Manchester M1 5FW
Tel: 0161 242 1406
Email: northwest@HistoricEngland.org.uk

South East
Eastgate Court
195-205 High Street
Guildford GU1 3EH
Tel: 01483 252020
Email: southeast@HistoricEngland.org.uk

South West
29 Queen Square
Bristol BS1 4ND
Tel: 0117 975 1308
Email: southwest@HistoricEngland.org.uk

Swindon
The Engine House
Fire Fly Avenue
Swindon SN2 2EH
Tel: 01793 445050
Email: swindon@HistoricEngland.org.uk

West Midlands
The Axis
10 Holliday Street
Birmingham B1 1TG
Tel: 0121 625 6870
Email: westmidlands@HistoricEngland.org.uk

Yorkshire
37 Tanner Row
York YO1 6WP
Tel: 01904 601948
Email: yorkshire@HistoricEngland.org.uk

We are the public body that looks after England's historic environment. We champion historic places, helping people understand, value and care for them.

Please contact
guidance@HistoricEngland.org.uk
with any questions about this document.

HistoricEngland.org.uk

If you would like this document in a different format, please contact our customer services department on:

Tel: 0370 333 0607
Fax: 01793 414926
Textphone: 0800 015 0174
Email: customers@HistoricEngland.org.uk

Please consider the environment before printing this document

HEAG067
Publication date: December 2004 © English Heritage
Reissue date: December 2015 © Historic England
Design: Historic England

Printed in Dunstable, United Kingdom